The Teaching for Social Justice Series

William Ayers
Series Editor

Therese Quinn
Associate Series Editor

Editorial Board: Hal Adams, Barbara Bowman, Lisa Delpit, Michelle Fine, Maxine Greene, Caroline Heller, Annette Henry, Asa Hilliard, Rashid Khalidi, Gloria Ladson-Billings, Charles Payne, Mark Perry, Luis Rodriguez, Jonathan Silin, William Watkins

---

Walking the Color Line: The Art and Practice of Anti-Racist Teaching
MARK PERRY

The Public Assault on America's Children: Poverty, Violence,
and Juvenile Injustice
VALERIE POLAKOW, EDITOR

Construction Sites: Excavating Race, Class, and Gender Among Urban Youths
LOIS WEIS AND MICHELLE FINE, EDITORS

A Simple Justice: The Challenge of Small Schools
WILLIAM AYERS, MICHAEL KLONSKY, AND GABRIELLE H. LYON, EDITORS

Holler If You Hear Me: The Education of a Teacher and His Students
GREGORY MICHIE

D0951689

WALKING THE COLOR LINE

The Art and Practice of Anti-Racist Teaching

MARK PERRY

Teachers College, Columbia University
New York and London

In Memory of Edward Brown, Fanon Nickerson,
Mark and Ragna Perry, and Laura Larsen

Published by Teachers College Press, 1234 Amsterdam Avenue, New York, NY 10027

Library of Congress Cataloging-in-Publication Data

Perry, Mark, 1948–
  Walking the color line : the art and practice of anti-racist teaching / Mark Perry.
    p. cm. — (The teaching for social justice series)
  Includes bibliographical references and index.
  ISBN 0-8077-3965-0 (cloth) — ISBN 0-8077-3964-2 (pbk.)
    1. Racism—Study and teaching—United States—Case studies. 2. Race relations—United States—Case studies. 3. Teaching—Social aspects—United States—Case studies. 4. Educational sociology—United States—Case studies. I. Title. II. Series.

  LC192.2 .P47 2000
  305.8'0071—dc21
                                                                        00-023416
ISBN 0-8077-3964-2 (paper)
ISBN 0-8077-3965-0 (cloth)

Printed on acid-free paper

Manufactured in the United States of America

07 06 05 04 03 02 01 00   8 7 6 5 4 3 2 1

Contents

Series Foreword

Teaching for social justice might be thought of as a kind of popular education—of, by, and for the people—something that lies at the heart of education in a democracy, education toward a more vital, more muscular democratic society. It can propel us toward action, away from complacency, reminding us of the powerful commitment, persistence, bravery, and triumphs of our justice-seeking forebears—women and men who sought to build a world that worked for us all. Abolitionists, suffragettes, labor organizers, civil rights activists: Without them, liberty would today be slighter, poorer, weaker—the American flag wrapped around an empty shell—a democracy of form and symbol over substance.

Rousseau argues in regard to justice that equality "must not be understood to mean that degrees of power and wealth should be exactly the same," but only that with respect to *power*, equality renders it "incapable of all violence" and only exerted in the interest of a freely developed and participatory law, and that with respect to *wealth*, "no citizen should be so opulent that he can buy another, and none so poor that he is constrained to sell himself." The quest for equality and social justice over many centuries is worked out in the open spaces of that proclamation, in the concrete struggles of human beings constructing and contesting all kinds of potential meanings within that ideal. Nothing is settled, surely, once and for all, but a different order of question presents itself: Who should be included? What do we owe one another? What is fair and unfair?

This series gathers together examples of popular education being practiced today, as well as clear and new thinking concerning issues of democracy, social justice, and educational activism. Many contributions will be grounded in practice and will, we hope, focus on the complexities built into popular education: difficulties, set-backs, successes, steps forward—work that reminds us of what Bernice Johnson

Reagon calls "the sweetness of struggle." We seek as well, developing theoretical work that might push us all forward as we labor to grasp anew the meaning of democracy in changing times, the demands of justice, and the imperatives of social change. We want to encourage new voices and new ideas, and in all cases to contribute to a serious, grounded, thoughtful exchange about the enduring questions in education: Education for what? Education for whom? Education toward what kind of social order?

If society cannot be changed under any circumstances, if there is nothing to be done, not even small and humble gestures toward something better, well, that about ends all conversation. Our sense of agency shrinks, our choices diminish. What more is there to say? But if a fairer, more sane, and just social order is both desirable and possible, that is, if some of us can join one another to imagine and build a participatory movement for justice, a public space for the enactment of democratic dreams, our field opens slightly. There would still be much to be done, for nothing would be entirely settled. We would still need to find ways to stir ourselves from passivity, cynicism, and despair; to reach beyond the superficial barriers that wall us off from one another; to resist the flattening effects of consumerism and the blinding, mystifying power of the familiar social evils (such as racism, sexism, and homophobia); to shake off the anesthesizing impact of most classrooms, most research, and of the authoritative, official voices that dominate the airwaves and the media; and to, as Maxine Greene says, "release our imaginations" and act on behalf of what the known demands, linking our conduit firmly to our consciousness. We would be moving, then, without guarantees, but with purpose and hope.

Education is an arena of struggle as well as hope—struggle because it stirs in us the need to look at the world anew, to question what we have created, to wonder what is worthwhile for human beings to know and experience—and hope because we gesture toward the future, toward the impending, toward the coming of the new. Education is where we ask how we might engage, enlarge, and change our lives, and it is, then, where we confront our dreams and fight our notions of the good life, where we try to comprehend, apprehend, or possibly even change the world. Education is contested space, a natural site of conflict—sometimes restrained, other times in full eruption—over questions of justice.

The work, of course, is never done. Democracy is dynamic, a community always in the making. Teaching for social justice continues the difficult task of constructing and reinvigorating a public. It broadens the table, so that more may sit together. Clearly, we have a long, long way to go. And we begin.

William Ayers, Series Editor
Therese Quinn, Associate Series Editor

Acknowledgments

Although they cannot be acknowledged by name, the many colleagues and students who crossed paths with this work, with their energy, ideas, and love, are its heart and soul and give it life and vibrancy. They made real a remarkable vision of alternative education and proved to themselves and others that academic excellence, critical introspection, and social action can transform learning and schooling for everyone.

I want to thank the generous people who gave freely of their time, knowledge, and insights in reading and critiquing earlier versions of this book and helped me navigate the road to renewed intellectual engagement: Susan Edgerton, who opened her heart, encouraged risk taking, and validated my journey into new learning experiences; Bill Schubert, who brought curriculum to life for me in unimaginable ways and left me always asking what is worthwhile to know and experience; Eleanor Binstock, who showed me how to maintain my humanity; Bill Ayers, who set me on the road to qualitative research and opened the door to publication; and Hal Adams, who provided needed political and practical grounding and whose work is a constant reminder of the truth and value of teaching for social justice.

I am sincerely grateful to three people who touched this work and my life in ways far greater than they realize: Sabrina Hope King, who listened when others turned away and jumped into the fray without ever looking for personal gain or platitudes; Annette Henry, who gave me perspective and encouragement and provided the soul and spice of life that kept me honest, hopeful, and able to keep charting my own road; and, although she must go unnamed, a colleague of many strengths who was both my sharpest critic and most constant support throughout 4 years of a life-changing experience that will forever impact our lives as educators.

On the long road of revision and rewrites, many thanks to Ann Berlock, who took time out of her busy life to offer up her thoughts and critique, and to Barbara Osbourne, who painstakingly read every page and wrote innumerable valuable comments. This book would not have seen the light of day without the support of Brian Ellerbeck from Teachers College Press, who stood with me every step of this process, including my personal strike against making any more changes and completing the manuscript. Lori Tate, also of Teachers College Press, and copyeditor Glorieux Dougherty both contributed extremely useful suggestions.

Lastly, it cannot go without saying that this work would have remained but an unshaped dream without the constant support, patience, and love of Meryl, Olivia, and Mila.

Introduction

Storytelling is central to my teaching and autobiography is the primary vehicle giving voice to my narratives. It is my entrance and pathway into observing, critiquing, and analyzing my role and actions as a teacher and it shapes my search for ways to talk and act on issues of race, culture, teaching, and learning.

This tale begins somewhere in my adolescence and culminates at Aztlan Alternative High School.

Tenth grade. The Kennedy-Nixon debate. Hearing the news of Kennedy's assassination during my 10th-grade geometry class and our ultraconservative teacher attempting to continue the day's lesson. A constant barrage of television images: *I Love Lucy* reruns; the *Ed Sullivan Show*; civil rights workers beaten by white men with baseball bats; bombings and killings in a small southeast Asian country I knew little about at the time. All of this clashing with my alcoholic parents' expectations that I be the first in the family to graduate from college, a changing body and blossoming sexuality that felt like an out-of-control roller coaster, and the threat of being drafted into the military.

High school for me was an obligation with little meaning. My recollections bring a range of feelings from anxiety to boredom. I ventured into conservative politics in 1964 as one of "Barry's Boys" because I thought Goldwater was honest. By 1966 my mind was in a tailspin, my grasp for direction up for grabs. My influences ranged from learning the world of work to the two young Black women in class who befriended me and told me they didn't think I believed what I was saying to my trip to the selective service office to register for the draft.

Outwardly I probably looked the same, but inside the eye of a hurricane yearned to break loose. Within a year of graduation, I'd taken a job at the post office, started college, got married, joined a group opposed to the draft, and marched in my first antiwar demonstration. Burned draft cards, demonstrations for Black Studies on campus, the birth of a son, the dissolution of the marriage, arrests at anti–Vietnam

War protests, the discovery of marijuana and psychedelics, and estrangement from my family seemed only to bring more questions and fewer answers. I didn't know it at the time, but the table was now set for a life-altering journey.

Hey, hey LBJ, how many kids did you kill today? Social justice; economic equality; an end to war, racism, and poverty. National liberation, cultural revolution, women's liberation, gay liberation. *Ho, Ho, Ho Chi Minh, the NLF are gonna win!* Marxism, socialism, armed struggle, guerrilla warfare, clandestine organizations. *Bring the War Home!* I pushed my limits personally and politically. Seven and one-half years underground led to entrapment in an FBI sting operation, a conspiracy indictment and conviction, and state prison. Initially facing over 40 years, I found that time stood still and I could only imagine the worst. My life began to lose focus. Was it my politics that got me here? Was I really pushing life to the limits or were the limits pushing me? My friends and I thought of ourselves as revolutionaries. Had we misjudged how to bring about real and lasting social change?

A combination of government misconduct, changing sentencing laws, and the human rights atmosphere of the newly elected Jimmy Carter administration led to a plea bargain and a 3-year sentence strongly objected to by the prosecution. With good time, I walked out of San Quentin Prison in 2 years. To this day, a part of me remains behind those bars—with Chino, doing life in the adjustment center in Folsom Prison; with Bo, murdered by guards and buried in a prison grave; with the many men I met working as the prisoner-teacher in the one-room schoolhouse at Susanville State Prison in Northern California.

As a teacher and researcher I think it is important to know something of the background of the person writing a book or article. While not necessarily a determining factor, it does influence how I judge the work. Is it important to know how I came to my present thinking? Will I be prejudged in ways that keep the reader from my work? And who really cares, as Marvin Gaye might say?

Prison was a life-changing experience, an epiphany of sorts, that fundamentally altered the way I view my position in the dominant white society. While I don't see myself as an exceptional white person, prison reshaped the lenses through which I view race, racism, and how we as whites can contribute positively to naming, opposing, and changing inequity and inequality. As a political prisoner, I was regarded with suspicion by most everyone. Harassed by the guards, not trusted by other whites, threatened constantly for associating with Black prisoners, held in medium to high security in every prison, I had an insider's view of life—one that few middle-class "educated" white folks seldom see. Humbled, yet empowered with a renewed will to work for social change, I now face the question: Can I translate these insights and experiences into lessons or reflections that will be of use?

My work with young people began as a teenager when I volunteered in a YMCA mentoring program. I had developed a love for learning and dreamed of someday teaching, although I swore to myself I would never be like the teachers I had when I was in school. I didn't have the formal opportunity to teach until I was assigned to the prison school working for a contracted teacher who seldom came to work. Ten years after leaving prison I finally earned a bachelor's degree. Later, a serendipitous congruence of alternative school teaching and meeting supportive academics led to graduate school and, eventually, teacher education. It wasn't until Aztlan Alternative High School that I found a place to work with others who shared similar, if not always identical, visions of popular, democratic, antiracist, progressive education. I am a believer because I witnessed it and participated in it firsthand.

This book represents the last 3 years of my 5 years at Aztlan Alternative High School. Part I, "Setting the Stage," introduces the school and gives a capsule summary of its history, leading up to a description of how students gained entrance and how the staff was structured. From here, I set some of the philosophical parameters that guide my work framed around two stories that serve as an example of how I weave my own observations into the conflicts that arose in the school. Part II, "The Aztlan Alternative Years," contains the narratives that shape and give life to the myriad questions and life experiences the school faced as we tried to bring democratic, antiracist education to life. Within this section, I have placed four Guideposts. Their intention is to explain the thematic connections and give coherence to the accumulated stories. Some readers may choose to skip over these interludes. Part III, "The Road Traveled: Creating an Engaged Pedagogy," places the narratives into a theoretical framework. While the narratives may stand alone for some, this section explains in more detail the hows and whys of the curriculum in use at Aztlan Alternative High School. It also addresses some of the pedagogical questions that may arise since so many of the stories have to do with the teachers and not with the many successes of the students.

After 5 years, Aztlan Alternative High School was forcefully, and some might say violently, disbanded by a new executive director of the agency overseeing the school. We didn't go without a fight but, as is described in the final sections, our *road traveled* often took odd turns because of the complexities of race. No longer solely a black/white or

Latino/white issue, nearly every debate had some kind of racial and political overtone.

Only I can take responsibility for the contents as well as the mistakes in this book. I changed the names and descriptions of all of the characters as well as the school's name and location. Any resemblance to the actual participants is reframed to change their identities. At the same time, all of the stories, debates, and dialogues come directly from copious notes and journal entries.

In the end, it is my hope that these pages translate into visions that encourage conversations and the sharing of stories without fear of retribution, the building of community, implementation of programs for social change, and the creation of new arenas to discuss honestly what it means to be white teachers, and to raise the standards and expectations for all teachers and students.

As a final note, I also present this work as a challenge to teacher education, in which all too often good ideas are taught traditionally. Even when the teaching is guided by progressive philosophies, the outcome becomes the creation of technicians taught to work either as generalists or as isolated, content-specific teachers. In too many cases, the teacher education programs themselves are administered as hierarchies and passive complicity becomes the modus operandi for faculty who become complacent or who fear losing their jobs. Are we willing to challenge this status quo and break the silence? As whites, we are the majority of teachers and teacher educators in an education system that is failing far too many children, especially children of color. Maybe what we are in need of is a crisis in consciousness. It is my hope that this work, while not a blueprint, might be a marker, and possibly a catalyst, on the long road of a life of learning and a world of peace, freedom, and social equality and justice.

PART I

SETTING THE STAGE

The boulevard. It's the tree-lined demilitarized zone of the neighborhood. The high school's policy of gang neutrality is severely tested on the 30-yard strips of grass that border both sides of the street. During the height of periodic gang conflicts, groups of young men play tag across the pavement, dodging passing cars, heaving bricks and bottles over passing car hoods, standing and posturing, calling out their gang names, throwing up their hands, two or three fingers raised high depending on which side of the street and which gang they represent.

Gang members attending Aztlan Alternative High School have to make a choice: participate and get kicked out of school, or walk away and get violated for not upholding the fidelity and reputation of their gangs. The more I heard their stories, the more I realized how hard it was to make that decision.

Hector and I stand by the school's main door. Sixteen years old and new to the school, he accuses me of not caring about him and wanting him to get hurt because I said it was against school policy to fight rival gang members in front of the school. "What about my honor?" he asks.

I don't know if I'll ever understand or appreciate either the uncompromising commitment or anger many of the young men feel toward each other. Rolando, 18, writes of his animosity toward a rival gang member:

> There is one person that you hate the most. This one person I hate with all my guts. This guy broke my windows a couple of times. He shot at me and I shot at him. I think I would go to jail just to kill this one person. That's how much I hate that person. I think the same thing goes for him.

Antonio, heavy set with a tattoo rising from his white T-shirt up his neck, has been a member of his gang for 11 years. He joined as a peewee and is now 18 and the father of a 5-month-old daughter. When he writes about his fellow gang members, it is with a strong sense of familial bonding:

> I care about my homeboys. Many thoughts have journeyed through my mind at the thought of losing one of my boys. I see everyone's faces and maybe tomorrow they won't be around to shake my hand or flame up a phillie with me. The sight of a dark car coming in my hood and releasing deadly lead and killing one of my homeboys is terrifying. Revenge would be the only answer.

I walk to the gravel parking lot around the corner at the end of the day or at night when I stay late. A young manchild passes me, gun in hand, casing the boulevard for his victim. I keep walking but I never cease to wonder why. Does he really believe revenge is the only answer?

I arrive again the next morning around 7:45, park in the lot, and walk through the alley past garage doors brightly painted with gang graffiti. Occasionally a homeowner paints out the insignias, but by the next morning someone has sprayed up a street-to-roof crown or pitchfork surrounded by a list of scrawled street names.

I enter the boulevard, grass glistening with dew, mothers protectively holding small hands as they walk their young children to the two local grammar schools. I forget about last night's gunshots, but I worry about the children. What makes some of them become their own worst enemies? As I round the alley corner, the school's murals rise as a monument to other solutions, to an inner peace and community awareness of drugs and violence. Two of the murals careen up three stories, preaching in bold Aztec and Mayan images the need for Mexican people to reconnect to their indigenous ancestry and use education as a tool for personal and collective liberation.

Entering the building through an enclosed rectangular room the size of a 6- by 12-foot holding cell, I am greeted by a mural covering the entire space. Corners disappear and faces merge into a spiral snake or a circular Mayan calendar. Every morning as I traverse this landscape, it is this mural that is my port of entry, my tunnel into learning that is built on a community tradition of resistance to the suicidal slaughter that sets up one young Latino against another, over a piece of turf.

AZTLAN ALTERNATIVE HIGH SCHOOL first opened its doors in the mid-1970s with 50 students. Located in a large urban Mexican-immigrant community in the Midwest, the school's first teachers were themselves students, activists from the Chicano Movement of the 1960s and 70s. Chicano historian Rudolfo Acuña (1981) describes the period as a time when Chicano youth set up their own organizations based in nationalism and a questioning of mainstream assimilation.

Aztlan Alternative was created as an alternative, culturally positive learning environment for public high school dropouts in the community. In 1978, the school philosophy focused on a curriculum that fostered the development of personal growth, student leadership, discipline, personal growth, and class and national consciousness. One of their primary goals was to help students become community activists. Reflecting the political mood of that time, they envisioned the school as a "model for the future in our larger communities of life."

Despite changes in staff, the Aztlan Alternative legacy continued, maintaining a continuum of practice. In 1989 a new teaching staff issued a reformulated school philosophy, based in the work of Brazilian educator Paulo Freire, that emphasized a practice where "educational theory and practice must be redefined in favor of the oppressed to begin to offset the uneven power relationships inherent in our society."

Throughout the years, a constant element of the school's tradition has been its commitment to empower young people to take responsibility for their own learning, to think critically, and to give back to their community. Recent graduate Isabel González wrote her personal reflections on how she feels about the school:

> The teachers and students are more like a family. That's why everybody calls each other by their first name. To call a teacher by their first name is straight because I can get along and talk to them like I would to my friends. It's very easy to talk about problems, either your own personal problems or problems with a teacher, what you do or don't like about their teaching, or just about anything so they can change to make it work for both of you.
>
> The reason this school works so well is because student opinion counts. Teachers really want to know how the students feel. Sometimes I look back at my counselors in public school where I had to call them Mrs. or Mr., where they never remembered my name, where I had to have an appointment to talk to them, where there was only one counselor for freshmen and sophomores. Anyway, they never really helped me with my problems. The teachers care if you're in school and when you're not, they worry about your education. They try their hardest to help you any way they can. Before I came to Aztlan Alternative I never even thought about college. I thought high school was enough.

Now I can't wait to go. Right here there is so much encouragement from the teachers that I feel like I can make it.

All of the teenagers who apply to Aztlan Alternative have left public school. Their reasons vary: alienation, violence, irrelevant classes,
parenthood, gang activity, lack of institutional support. To get into the
school they have to fill out an application and attend an orientation
with a parent or a responsible adult in their lives. The next day, they
come, by themselves, to an interview with two teachers and two students. The interview is a grueling process and one I don't know if I
could have survived as a 16-year-old. The prospective students must
convince us that they want to be back in school.

The teaching staff is a cooperative. We attempt to make all major
decisions through a democratic process of discussion and consensus
building. We don't agree all of the time and sometimes we vote just
because we have to move ahead, but there is no supreme authority
or boss that dictates policy. We meet in smaller curricular groups to
discuss classes and share syllabi and lessons. Students write self-
evaluations every 6 weeks; we respond with written and oral evaluations and engage in individual and class conversations to talk about
needed changes. Students critique the entire school and meet with
staff and teachers individually to assess how we are meeting their academic and personal needs.

Classes are small, ranging from 12 to 20 students, depending on
the subject area. Each teacher is responsible for an advisory group of
12 to 14 students. They meet daily and discuss school and personal
issues. The advisory group serves as a support mechanism and remains
together throughout a student's stay in the school. Class management
is a relative nonissue at Aztlan Alternative. Self-discipline, peer discussion, and democratic participation replace the security guards and detention rooms found in most of the city's public high schools. School
rules are created jointly by students and teachers. We meet weekly in
an assembly/school meeting where anyone can raise issues that impact
the school. We talk openly about gangs, sexuality, race, gender, homophobia, and any other issue that teachers or students want to bring
up. We bring in speakers and cultural performers, and celebrate special
events and holidays with student/teacher potlucks and ceremonies led
by an indigenous Chicano elder on staff.

Aztlan Alternative works! Well, not always, but it never lacks for
excitement and an electrifying enthusiasm about learning. The majority of students, while not necessarily enjoying public school, did not
voluntarily leave. They were rejected, spit out like pieces of moldy

food, by a system that cannot or will not listen to them or meet their needs. Many have been impacted by violence, gangs, pregnancies, teen parenthood, drugs, alcohol, dysfunctional and abusive families and relationships, racism, and poverty; yet all are survivors who have made a conscious choice to continue their high school education. Aztlan Alternative looks for the positives in their lives: personal strengths, family histories and support networks, community cohesion, and ethnic and individual identity. It places a high priority on language with both Spanish and English taught as language arts. The teaching staff is committed to developing and implementing an innovative, interdisciplinary, student-centered, and culturally relevant curriculum as part of creating a space where students feel wanted, respected, and academically and personally challenged.

Above all, Aztlan Alternative offers a safe, student-positive environment. The closest local high school is renowned as one of the worst in the city academically, as well as being riddled with constant gang and racial violence. Aztlan Alternative is an open campus and violence-free. We have no metal detectors and rival gang members attend classes together. Individuality, student opinion, and choice are respected. Students are valued as young adults transitioning into full adulthood with all its incumbent responsibilities. Half of the female students are mothers. Before we set up on-site child care for students' children and an after-school support group, young mothers seldom graduated. During the last 3 years, since the addition of child care, over half the graduates have been teen mothers.

I love this school—the students, the teachers, the overall ambience and feeling of pride in self and community. It was excruciatingly painful to say good-bye. I cried with other teachers and students the day of our final assembly. The new powers that controlled the agency that oversees the high school no longer supported our work or the direction we had charted for the school. In the end, our teachers, philosophy, and curriculum were pushed out just like our students had been from their previous schools. I had never before experienced as dynamic a learning or work situation as the one I lived at Aztlan Alternative High School.

SO, WHO AM I? How did I get here at Aztlan Alternative High School? Is it even appropriate that I work or teach in this school? Where are the voices of the Latino/Mexican students, teachers, and administrators in this narrative? How did I become a supervisor of teachers, a coordinator/principal of a school with an evolving Mexican-centric curricular philosophy? Is there a role for whites in a predominantly Latino school and if there is, how can I justify my role as both teacher and supervisor? In chronicling my experiences, how do I factor in my preconceived ideas? Through whose eyes am I seeing? Is it possible to accurately observe and translate others' experiences through my experiences? If not, how do I create relationships built on trust that can provide honest responses without being just another white person coming in and then leaving?

I always felt perplexed and concerned about my multiple roles as teacher, counselor, administrator, observer, friend, and researcher. Issues of race, ethnicity, racism, culture, and identity were ever-present and I needed to be an active, full participant in the life of the school. But I have also seen too many whites take a color-blind approach to working with people of color, which inevitably ended up with the whites making judgments and decisions based on their (white) experiences. Issues of privilege and authority end up transcending a search for more honest solutions based on the needs of the participants of color as well as the real, as opposed to perceived, needs of whites.

Hardly a day went by when I did not question why I was there at Aztlan Alternative. I constantly found myself asking: Is it possible for a white person, and a white man in particular, to be effective or of use as a teacher and administrator in a school populated with students and staff of color? Who are we, these white educators/professionals? What is our role? Can we be good at what we do, be part of a collaborative process, and be of use? With these questions in mind, I present the first stories.

BETTY

I pull up an extra chair and sit in the office of Sylvia Fuentes, the director of education who oversees the agency's high school and adult education programs. She is a self-defined Chicana who carries herself with a streetwise professionalism. It is one of those sweltering September days that makes you wonder if the ozone layer has finally evaporated into the atmosphere. Sweat rolls over my ribs from the humidity and the tension as I watch and listen to Betty Wilmington, the white administrator of a citywide arts organization, explain why her program should not be held accountable to the students, staff, or curriculum of our high school.

Aztlan Alternative has been working with Betty's group for 8 years. Teachers hired by her taught a video and media arts class and trained students to use equipment at the local cable access studio. On behalf of the high school, I had been in discussions with her and her staff since spring. We talked about student criticisms of their classes and curricular content, and I presented a proposal asking that we be more involved in the hiring process of the video arts teacher. While initially friendly, our conversations turned ugly. I was beginning to feel that their main objective was to use Aztlan Alternative students as bodies in their grant proposals.

The issue was further complicated by the fact that they maintained an off-site office in the school and their entire video arts staff was white. So here I was, this white administrator negotiating with the white woman executive director and her white staff about their relationship to a Latino school. I wanted to change the dynamics. I asked Betty to meet with Sylvia and me to see what we could work out.

"You are not respecting my status and the 20 years I have given to the Latino community," Betty stated, sitting rigid in her chair. She became increasingly agitated as the discussion progressed, and continued by describing to Sylvia and me how she has done more for Latinos in the arts than anyone else in the city and how the community and this high school "owes" her for her work.

At first I felt bad for Betty, but my empathy soon turned to pity and embarrassment. She told us that she was ahead of her time and that by requesting changes in her program we were interfering in what she knew was best for our students. We tried to offer a compromise and suggested a more cooperative relationship with her program where students would still have the opportunity to work with her outside of class, but she refused. Betty insisted on their classes' being fully implemented, without input or changes. The word *racism* hovered, unspoken, over our entire conversation. I left the discussion feeling that if I ever get like this—the disgruntled white authority figure who knows best—take me away and put me out of everyone's misery.

In part, this incident points to a dilemma facing progressive whites whose self-image is based on "how much I have contributed to communities of color." Because Betty believes the community owes her for her commitment and her work, she also thinks her special relationship gives her the right and expectation to be a participant, in her words, in all "high-level" discussions.

Betty is not a bad person. In fact, she has devoted over 20 years of her life to "empowerment" of people of color and "fighting racism." Her work with the high school started when a progressive and effective white male headed this not-for-profit, community-based agency. For the dozen years he ran the agency, funding increased and the high school and related social service programs grew. The board of directors made a political decision to hire a Latino executive director and transfer authority and decision-making to a management team staffed by Latinos. During the transition, it was made clear to Betty that all ongoing and continuing relationships would be discussed and reviewed.

At what point did Betty's *special relationship* break down? And, more importantly, who was *special* in the relationship? During the negotiations, she verbally accepted our request to be part of the hiring process for her staff. The only problem was that she hired a white male and *then* asked for a date when the high school could interview him as the new video arts teacher. They were both told that he could only be a candidate, even though he was already under the employ of her arts agency. As a conciliatory gesture, the full high school staff interviewed her candidate and he was unanimously found unacceptable. This still didn't dissuade Betty from keeping him. As the dialogue was breaking down, I asked Betty why, since the inception of the arts program 8 years ago, there had only been one teacher of color hired to teach here. She replied that they interview 20 to 30 applicants each year and that it has been "difficult" to find qualified people of color.

Sounds familiar. At the previous alternative and predominantly African-American school where I had worked, the all-white administration rationalized the lack of Black teaching staff (one in 17 years) as a case of "not being able to find qualified Black teachers."

FROM THE FRYING PAN INTO THE FIRE

After the meeting with Betty, the relationship with the arts program was terminated. The high school decided to develop its own, independent project. We went on a search for a new video arts teacher. Issues of race again flared up when we tried to make a decision. We interviewed two candidates. One was Darnell Peck, a young white man who had previously worked part-time in Betty's program. He was well liked by the students, who felt that he listened to their ideas. The second candidate was Irma Betances, a Puerto Rican woman and independent filmmaker. Darnell was characterized as stable, steady, and a good technician who could slowly rebuild the program. Irma was spoken of as creative, Latina, more experienced in filmmaking, but with less access to resources and more of an unknown as a teacher.

Staff split evenly—equal numbers of Latinos and whites for each candidate. Then the bloodletting began. No one was willing to budge. Positions got harder and tempers rose. Race and commitment became the main issues. Sal de la Luz, a Puerto Rican who teaches Spanish and history, raised the hairs on Patrice Trumbell's neck when he said he could never live with himself if we hired a white guy over a Latina. Patrice, who is one of the few white graduates of the school and now works as the registrar, responded that if that were true then she should just leave and let a Latina be hired in her position. She said she was disgusted with us and how we seem to use different standards for different people depending on their race.

Elena Hernández, who teaches Spanish and English language arts, tried to get us back on track by focusing more on the direction of the video arts program when Alberto Carmona, our Chicano elder, unkindly compared Irma to a lesbian who had previously worked at the school for 10 years. Up to that point, Irma's sexual orientation had not been an issue. The room polarized. We asked Sylvia to join us. For her, gender was the most important qualifier and, if the issue was short-term stability versus a more creative direction, she fell on the creativity side.

In our effort to resolve staff disagreements through discussion and consensus, we sought common ground. Except for reluctant agreement from Patrice and Alberto, we decided to hire Irma.

LOOKING BACK at the episode with Betty, I was pushed to further rethink my own actions as a white educator working with people of color. I remarked to a friend that what scared me most about the conversations with Betty was that, if circumstances were different, I could see myself in her shoes. I saw the enemy and he was white. White progressives, white liberals, white radicals: The operative word is white. Although I like to think I have wrestled with some of these racial problematics, the questions and questioning are ongoing and complacency can easily become a cancer. I relate both of these episodes because they are points of entry in which to examine white educators and our working relationships with students, teachers, and administrators of color.

Where to begin? One essential marking point is that the frames of reference are not the same for white teachers. Too often, we refuse to acknowledge the message or even see the messenger. We seldom challenge or question each other about racism. It's not that we can't be heard proclaiming loudly our interest in hearing from people of color or quoting from the newest literary work or research from an author or scholar of color. The *problem* arises when people of color are critical or even just offer another point of view. This is when white folks become defensive and protective and fall back on stereotypic responses like "but I've done so much for the (fill in the blank) community" and "I'm a good teacher; why would a (fill in the nationality) teacher be better in this class?" As in Betty's case, this is not only a different frame of reference. These are the wrong questions.

Empowerment necessitates change, which necessitates a fresh look at established relationships. Now in my late 40s, I find it necessary to reexamine and redefine many accepted structures and assumptions. The stark difference, most frequently witnessed in urban education, between who is a student in a class and who teaches the class leads me to re-question the role of white teachers. Who are we? Where do we come from? What are our motives? Is race neutrality possible or even desirable in the classroom? Are there alternative ways of being and teaching? As white teachers, can we begin to ask ourselves the kinds of questions, or do we even know the questions to ask, that will allow us to learn from and be in more dialogue with teachers of color, students of color and their parents, and each other? Can we be more responsive, can we challenge our own frames of references without relying solely on people of color to ask the questions? Are we truly willing to participate in open, honest dialogue?

At one point when I was trying to explain to Betty Wilmington my view of what had happened vis-à-vis her arts program, how I felt, and what I thought I was learning as a white teacher at this school, she said it was not her responsibility to initiate the discussions about her program. Aside from the fact that she had not previously understood that her program's relationship was being questioned, she did not perceive any responsibility, as a white person working in a community of color, to continually ask herself the hard questions about race, privilege, equality, her role as a white person, or how and in what ways she is accountable to that community.

MY FIRST YEAR at Aztlan Alternative was one of transition. I had applied to work at the high school at the invitation of the Chicano director of the program. I was immediately pulled into the racial dynamics of the staff, which at that time was polarized into three camps: the whites and two groups of Latinos. At Alberto Carmona's urging, I met separately a few times with the white teachers. All had come to the school as some form of religious service and missionary commitment and had an extremely difficult time seeing race as an issue. They saw themselves as nonracist (as opposed to antiracist) and felt that one of the biggest problems was prejudice against them by the Latino staff. Personality conflicts kept the Latino teachers divided and led to many of the Latino staff leaving at the end of the year.

That spring, as the school year came to a close, I was asked by two of the Latina staff to apply to become the new coordinator/principal. I told them I didn't want the position and that I thought it would be more appropriate to try to find a Latino coordinator. They agreed, but told me I would be the best person right now for the school. After a number of Latino candidates were interviewed, I was again asked to apply. I interviewed with administration, students, and staff. At the final staff interview, Sal and Alberto said I was qualified and would do a good job, but they wanted a Latino in the position. I took myself out as a candidate although the two staff who had initially encouraged me did not agree with this decision. After subsequent interviews, all four Latino staff approached me to reconsider. I agreed to take the position as long as we had agreement that the staff would continue to function as a cooperative and that I would do it for only 2 years.

I embarked on my new position with hope marked by ambivalence and apprehension, including Sal telling me he still did not know if he could work "under" a white person. He did say I would be "better than a fascist Latino." I tried to redefine the position to accommodate his concerns, but being the white guy in *authority*, I never felt comfortable as a supervisor.

I did not enter Aztlan Alternative as a researcher and it was never my main function. It was a role that evolved over time and started a year after I accepted the position of coordinator/principal. Looking back at my first journal entries, it is clear that I didn't foresee it as a 3-year journey. I did sense that functioning as teacher, administrator, participant, and researcher, and immersing myself in the life of the school, opened doors that could not have been otherwise revealed or opened.

Who am I, who are we, these white teachers who choose to teach students of color? Are our responsibilities any different from those of other teachers? What does it mean when we are the only white faces in the classroom? How does this impact on our work with colleagues who are teachers and administrators of color? This inquiry and the stories that follow begin to probe these questions. I have not set out to present formulas, blueprints, or ultimate truths for being effective antiracist white teachers. At the same time, I do hope this narrative helps others, especially white teachers, reflect on our views and practices. It matters what we do and how we think.

PART II

THE AZTLAN
ALTERNATIVE YEARS

Guidepost

The Aztlan Alternative stories begin at the start of my 3rd year of teaching and my 2nd year as principal at the school. Looking in on our initial staff meeting of the year, we meet the teachers and the agency's new director of education, Sylvia Fuentes. Our main thematic focuses are student-centered curriculum, multilevel classes, and accountability. Early discussions lead us quickly into issues of identity, language, and the role of politics in the curriculum. Additionally, multiculturalism raised itself as an issue in subsequent meetings as we battled to stay unified in purpose while forthright in our commitment to putting our differences on the table. Tensions reached a crescendo during debate on the school's approach to and participation in activities marking the quincentennial of Columbus' arrival.

Looking back, I now see this as a transition year. Early on I agree to continue as principal and full-time teacher and Sylvia takes over the day-to-day supervisorial responsibilities in an effort to alleviate some of the animosities among the staff to there being a white principal. While this move was partially successful, this was an issue that would continue into the next year even though nearly half the staff would be new to the school.

These first stories chronicle some of my interactions with students as well as teachers and culminate with the biggest challenge yet to hit the high school. Since its inception in the mid-1970s, the high school had maintained a certain autonomy with the overall agency even as the agency grew to become a multimillion-dollar community-based social services organization. When a noneducator took over as executive director, he sought to disband our on-site child-care center for student mothers and fire Sylvia. Mobilizing within the agency and the community, the high school led a 3-week strike that culminated with the board of directors changing the building's locks, calling in the police, and firing me and other teachers. A student encampment, midnight negotiations, a threatened building takeover, and continuous public, democratic meetings on the boulevard in front of the school led us to victory and a large community celebration.

1

The School Year Begins

We sit together at four round tables in what we call our library, its tattered books sitting on student-made wooden bookshelves. The years-old encyclopedias peer down at us with their missing volumes staring out like lost teeth. The third-floor room sits at the corner of this formally abandoned apartment building, rehabbed through a student carpentry program. Pleasant in the winter as it looks out on leafless trees and smoke wafting from nearby chimneys, it is a living hell in hot weather. The street traffic and winds collide and you can't hear yourself think. Today is one of those end-of-summer pleasant days that makes you forget the humidity and cherish thoughts of the upcoming fall.

There is very little staff turnover this year and the agency's got Sylvia Fuentes as its new director of education. A Chicana in her late 30s, she came here from California as a labor organizer nearly 15 years ago. We've made some wholesale changes in classes this year and it looks like the staff is reenergized, which is good, because we had seemed to run out of gas by the end of last June.

Alberto Carmona is our staff elder. Leather faced, he's in his mid-50s and fond of short-sleeve political T-shirts, even in the coldest weather. He's been here 13 years. He self-identifies as indigenous Chicano and tells us that over the summer Native American elders in his community told him he needs to speak out more. In this spirit, Alberto says the school does not belong to one person or group of people with their own agendas or turf. He points out what he perceives as a "doing our own thing mentality" permeating the staff. He wants us to talk with each other more and do activities together.

Elena Hernández is starting her 2nd year. Elena carries herself with an air of spirituality. On the days she lets her long hair hang loose, it floats in every direction, creating an aura of gentleness as she moves about her classes. When Elena first interviewed for a teaching position, she was impressed by the school's big windows. The physical presence of the building left her with a sense of capability. Elena is looking to build on the positive, question our class schedule, and reconsider our ideas about how and what we teach.

Patrice Trumbell is an Aztlan Alternative graduate and works as the registrar. She's white, grew up in this community, and speaks fluent Spanish. She has a 2-year-old son and is recently divorced from her Mexican husband. Patrice and Elena are proposing that we institute a home room and begin each school day with a ceremony or spiritual circle.

Altogether, we're beginning this year with a large staff—eight teachers, plus Patrice, Sylvia, and myself. Last year's staff theme was unity within diversity. This year we are focusing on fully implementing a student-centered curriculum and revisiting the relationship between politics and curriculum.

We begin our first week of meetings by asking ourselves four questions:

1. How do we name a process that accurately begins with the interests of the students?
2. What are the problems and issues our students are concerned about?
3. How do we develop a sense of purpose from the out-of-school experiences of the students?
4. What motivates someone to learn?

Implementing a student-centered curriculum is verbally accepted, but not fully embraced by all the staff. Robert Swindell is one of our English language arts teachers. He came to Aztlan Alternative 4 years ago as part of a religious community service commitment, working his 1st year as a volunteer. He feels strongly that we should not continue our discussions about student-centered curriculum outside the presence of students. Paul Prestonovich, tall, lanky, an avid basketball and frisbee player, and another former religious volunteer, suggests that we keep the same schedule of classes and put all other changes on hold until the start of winter session so we can engage these questions more fully with the students. Robert and Paul are the longest-standing white teachers in the school. Paul was Patrice's student advisor and has been with the program 9 years. While their ideas about involving students are not unreasonable, most of the staff feel we need to take responsibility as teachers in creating an environment that can facilitate change. We know the students well enough to gauge where we can create new forums and structures within the school.

Two and a half days of discussion leave us with another question:

Given that half the staff is white, how far can we go in building and facilitating the search for identity with students?

We begin by adding Indigenous Studies, taught by Alberto, and Women's Studies with Elena, and restructuring the Spanish-language program as language arts, breaking from the traditional format of Spanish taught as a foreign language. In a sweeping change, we propose making all classes multilevel. This includes creating core Spanish and English language arts classes that focus on literacy and reading. Elena and I also initiated a separate bilingual writing program outside the core classes.

By the end of the second week, cracks are beginning to surface among staff. Even while Alberto encourages us to air our true feelings and differences and get emotional, we are starting to lose some of our sense of unity of purpose. One of the administrative and structural problems we face is documenting our work, both for funders of the school and for our own evaluatory procedures. I presented an overview of our need for more accountability with each other, the students, the community, and our funders. It was met with a wall of silence. We talk about dialogic education and cooperative learning, and then half the staff sits back and doesn't participate in discussions. I have the feeling that staff as a whole is feeling: Fine, let him propose systems of accountability, but they'll never work. The proposals aren't radical. It's a matter of documenting what we do with our classes and structuring in time for preparation, discussion, and reflection.

Alberto is the first to raise time as an issue. He is followed by Jane Larsen, a former English as a Second Language teacher and a blond Scandinavian who speaks fluent Spanish. She was transferred into the high school from another part of the agency to be an additional English language arts teacher. "We don't have enough time now and there is no time for follow-up with students or other teachers." Sal de la Luz, tall, classically handsome, openly gay, and the only Puerto Rican on staff, added, "We don't have time to do what we want to do as it is. We don't get paid enough anyway."

All of their issues are reasonable but they are presented in a collective whine. Being a staff cooperative has its benefits, but it's times like these that I understand the reason for hierarchical decision-making. But, since that is not our bent, we persevere and decide to focus on practical ways to document our teaching and make time for more staff discussions.

The biggest internal problem I see as we begin a new school year is the passive aggressiveness among some of the staff in reaction to the new changes. Except for Elena, the language arts teachers are trying to portray themselves more as victims than as teachers embarking on new pedagogical thresholds. Robert questioned all the proposed changes. He said they would confuse students, teachers wouldn't be prepared, and "the English language arts program isn't supported enough by the rest of the staff." Robert is the only teacher who thinks the students will not embrace these changes. Sal and Elena spoke to how the Spanish program already began this transition last year. I mentioned how the writing program went through similar changes by involving students in the process of examining and changing our approach to teaching writing, although we have not talked enough about this with the whole staff or acknowledged it in the curriculum.

The Spanish language arts discussion focused on issues of bilingualism, cultural genocide, and respect for the community. We reaffirmed the need for Spanish as a central component of the program, although we differed on how to break out the classes. Sal held to the idea that, while change is necessary, we shouldn't change too fast. Sylvia challenged this notion by proposing that we do away with Spanish I, II, III and name our classes literature, drama, and writing without feeling we have to stay in a traditional format. Elena argued for the establishment of an ongoing Spanish as a Second Language class for students not yet ready to enter the full Spanish program.

The final step in our preparations is interviewing new student applicants. They fill out an application, come to an orientation with a parent or a responsible adult, and, the following day, come on their own for an interview with two staff and two students. If they miss any step, they are automatically deferred to the next session. The interviews tend to be overly subjective, but they give us a chance to see if we think the student is ready to be back in school. It gives the applicants the opportunity to learn more and to see if this school fits their needs. At the end of each interview the students and teachers discuss the applicant and make a recommendation to the full staff. This year, we begin with 79 students. We are debating trying to have an enrollment of 90 at the start of winter session in January.

Three weeks of meetings are beginning to fray everyone's nerves. It's a good thing classes start Monday. We're always much better when we're in the classroom and with students. Some of the teachers were starting to freak, feeling unprepared, but we go through this every year. Overall, there is an upbeat feeling. Patrice set up a bulletin board at the top of the stairs welcoming students as they enter the student lounge. Most of us have already talked with our advisees one-to-one over the phone or here at school.

A WEEK AFTER classes started, Alberto and Sal presented a proposal in the staff meeting. They want the school to participate in anti-Columbus demonstrations marking the quincentennial, the 500 years since the arrival of the Europeans. There was immediate agreement until the issue became whether participation would be voluntary or mandatory. Our pedagogical philosophy leads us to teach from the viewpoint of the marginalized and the oppressed. Based on early Paulo Freire, we look to find the words and deeds of those who resisted the European conquest. Unfortunately, the social studies teachers tend to see their subject areas as the only place where radical content is taught. The other disciplines are looked at as secondary to the "real" classes, such as Chicano Studies, Contemporary History, and Political Science.

I wanted the school to participate, but I urged us to do an education campaign that included allowing students to choose whether to go to the protest. I was severely criticized by Alberto and Sal. Alberto said the staff is not supporting him and I am counterpoising curriculum to the need to focus on the 500 years of resistance. He talked about his life as a Chicano and growing up in this city. Discovering his indigenous being has brought him in touch with a deeper convergence of his dual identities. He challenged me and the other white staff: "I feel racism right here in this room, at this school. This is not an issue for outsiders to decide, especially whites, even ones who temporarily live in the community."

This did not turn out to be a clean white/Latino split. The Latina staff all voiced strong opinions in favor of voluntary participation. The issue was further complicated by an undercurrent of debate concerning the projection of the counter-demonstrations. Were they the project of a single political tendency or an honest attempt to unify progressives in opposition to the genocide inherent in celebrating Columbus as a hero? The discussions are heated and, at times, antagonistic. We agreed to talk about the political issues in our classes and present an all-school educational, our version of a 1960s teach-in where speakers and performers come to the school to address a specific topic.

Students responded positively to the ideas presented in class. The educational became a day of culture with poets and Native drummers followed by a fiesta of indigenous foods. The low point for some of the staff was the keynote speaker, who was announced as a cultural worker but proceeded to give a lengthy advertisement for the political agenda of the counter march.

Since staff could not agree, we had to make participation at the demonstration voluntary and most students elected to attend. We gathered on October 12 outside the school and waited for our rented buses. The protest was characterized by loud chanting and marching in the streets with police walking side by side with the demonstrators. Walking back to our buses after the march, we stopped to watch the official parade. It turned out to be the highlight of our day. Although it had been projected in the media as a cross-cultural celebration, what we saw was worse than any of us expected. After a leading contingent of Native Americans, the parade was white and Italian, one group after another, marching bands and Boy Scouts. Students responded with oppositional chants and discussions among themselves about what they were witnessing.

Ironically, we would not have attended the official march if our buses had not been stuck among the hundreds of others bringing participants to the parade route. It turned out to be a more powerful educational experience for the students than just attending the counter march. This reaffirmed for me a belief in the need to involve students earlier in our discussions. They would have benefited by having to develop their own opinions without the gut check of being told this was the correct thing to do.

Two days later Sal announced he was quitting Aztlan Alternative in December to teach at a public high school in a nearby Puerto Rican neighborhood at a salary $10,000 more than he is making here. His decision was impacted by the Columbus Day debates and his desire to work more closely with the political organization responsible for the counter march. The students were disappointed and accused him of selling out, calling him a traitor. We defended Sal's decision at the assembly. Students loosened up and spoke of how much they'll miss him. We now have to begin the search for a new Spanish teacher.

I USED THE "M" WORD TODAY in staff meeting: *multiculturalism.* Boy did I get shot down. It began as a discussion of bilingual education. We talked about the various types of bilingual programs—transitional, maintenance, and immersion—and what we want for our school. There is agreement on the need for a full component of English and Spanish. Ideally, students will be fluent and literate in both languages. This led into a discussion of the relationship of language and race. Sal emphasized the pain students feel about their language. He used himself as an example. Born and raised in a nearby neighborhood, he did not learn Spanish until he was in college. Irma Betances, our new video arts teacher, responded that this was about much more than language. "It has to do with a whole spectrum of feelings that you have to be better than whites just to be up to par with them."

I made the point that some educators now refer to Black English and standard English as a form of bilingualism and threw out the phrases Afrocentric and Latino-centric multiculturalism. This set off a firestorm, mainly critical of multiculturalism as an assimilationist strategy promoting a melting-pot viewpoint that negates differences and elevates the dominant white culture as naturally superior. The discussion quickly turned to the question of the role of white staff.

Alberto, when asked by other Chicanos why the school has white staff, said he was caught off guard and became apologetic. "Blacks would never have white staff or be multicultural," he said. "It isn't personal about the whites on staff."

Maria Villamontes, a Chicana in her early 20s, tentative and tearful, stated that she felt divisions among the Latino staff. "They are unspoken. We look like we're a block and we end up talking down to the white teachers." Edgar Renta, our science teacher, added, "I am tired of being Latino-baited. I feel my Latinoness is called into question if I don't agree with the other Latinos on staff."

Passions rose. Irma leaned forward in her chair. "The main reason I was hired was because I am a Latina, not on my qualifications." Elena and I both disagreed, but in truth it was a factor, as was the fact that she is a lesbian. We also believed she was the best qualified.

I tried to clarify what I meant by multiculturalism, but I only stuck my foot further in my mouth. "When multiculturalism is linked to a centric pedagogy, it places it in a different framework. It can then challenge power relationships. This puts it more in the framework of cultural relevancy." I told Alberto it *was* personal for me, as well as being ideological. "I question every day what I'm doing here and whether I should even be at this school. I would hope all the white staff keep this as an open question in their minds."

Alberto concluded our discussion by saying that he was pleased we could have this kind of talk and he wanted more, but I didn't know how much further we could go. Most of the white staff were silent and I didn't believe there was enough trust among the Latino staff to fully have this kind of discussion with the white staff in the room. Sylvia added later that she was upset with Maria and Edgar for trying to play the role of brokers for the white staff. She was also vehement in criticizing the white staff who said nothing. "They watch the Latinos battle it out, feeling like they are above it all."

IN ONE OF the few quiet moments I have at my desk, I've been meditating on what makes this place work. I think it comes down to the unspoken intangibles, those things not in the job descriptions that go unrecognized and unnamed—Patrice talking to the mother of a student in Spanish and assuring her that her daughter is a good mother to her young child; Alberto burning sage and holding a ceremonial circle with students; Robert wearing his funky ties.

I notice it most on the days when I'm not standing at the top of the stairs or standing in front of the school when students arrive in the morning. Students ask me what I've been doing and jokingly say they wouldn't go to class if I wasn't there prodding them along.

SYLVIA ASKED ME to come talk with her this morning. "We need to talk about your plans for next year. Are you open to another year as principal?" Even though I'd emphatically said I would not do the job for more than 2 years, I'm open to another year if staff are agreeable. I'm generally pleased with what we've accomplished and I'm challenged with how much further I think we can go. My biggest hesitation is still the contradiction of being the *white principal*.

I see the high school staff changing and the possibility, really for the first time next year, of having a hand-picked and collectively chosen group of qualified teachers. This excites me. Already, in just the past 2 years, many of the teachers who had been here up to 10 years have left and a new group is in the process of developing. Sylvia's approach, which I have come to agree with, is to make whatever changes we can this year in light of starting up anew and strong next fall.

One of the areas to be worked on is the salary scale. Most of the staff, myself included, have been jerked around by the administration in one way or another. Plus, we're grossly underpaid, especially the experienced teachers. Quite honestly, I think most people wouldn't work for what we're paid when the starting pay for newly certified teachers is over $10,000 higher in the public schools. It takes a special commitment to be here, but people still have to be justly compensated.

Curricularly, I want us to keep growing while we try to institutionalize (in a good way) some of the changes we've already made. The internal development of the staff is another area that's exciting because we're creating the process ourselves. There's no real authority standing above us, dictating to us. We have quite a bit of leeway to experiment. As long as we keep moving forward, it feels good.

One question on the floor, and maybe we need another changeover in staff to make it real, is how to balance the freedom to create curriculum and involve students in developing lessons with the responsibility of completing the mundane tasks of running a quality program. Since we don't have a typical supervisor or principal, where are the mechanisms within a cooperative staff that can assure accountability to the students as well as the funders?

My job has begun to feel more like that of a curriculum coordinator. I also have a full teaching schedule. I realize that I can't do both well and it is the supervisorial duties that suffer most. Part of it, I know, is avoidance on my part because of the racial dynamic. Even though I am trying to redefine what it means to be a supervisor within a cooperative structure, it has been made clear to me by some of the Latino staff that they don't want a white guy being their supervisor. I thought the idea of an honor system and peer accountability would solve the problem, but it's not working. What gets lost is the accountability.

Sylvia and I are going to propose that she take over the supervisorial responsibilities, including making sure staff get their paperwork completed and arrive at class on time. Part of me feels this is a cop-out, but at least the oppositional racial dynamic with the Latino staff won't be in the mix. I wonder what the white staff will think about this change? It's not as though the accountability is working for them either.

2

Anthony

As I sit at my desk before first period, the phone rings. "This is Mark," I answer. It's Anthony's mother. He's one of my new advisees this year. "Anthony's father threw him out of the house last night. Will you talk with him?" I tell her I'll go look for him.

Seventeen and thin as a broom handle, Anthony has little money, no job, and he and his girlfriend, Ana, have a 1-year-old daughter. His father came home drunk again last night and they argued. He says his father's drinking is driving his mother out too. I ask him if he'd like me to try and set him up in the agency's transitional living program. He says yes.

We talk a lot about gangs in the school. Most everyone knows who is and who isn't a gang member. I stay away from asking explicitly about any individual's activities and affiliations. Students are required to keep their gang activities out of the school, including representing with their colors, clothes, or hand signs, but Anthony wanted to talk. So I listened. He told me he was a former member who'd lost his status after making a move on a fellow gang member's girlfriend. A dozen members of his own gang confronted him at his home. He and his father, a long-time member in the gang, met them at the front door. A fight ensued and Anthony's father got stabbed twice. He then shot one of the guys on his porch. The police came, followed by a local television crew. Anthony spoke on camera and was subsequently confronted again, this time for going public with gang business. He was told he couldn't wear his colors or represent in the street.

Anthony is currently out on bail for attempted murder in another incident, in which he hit a guy with a brick who looked at Ana. He doesn't deny this. It was Ana who turned him in.

Anthony's doing okay in his transition back to school. He's been out for nearly 2 years. His reading is at a sixth-grade level. He is expressive and generally stays focused in the classroom. He is clearly rough around the edges and, from what I've heard, has a violent temper. Ana has been attending Aztlan Alternative for a year and supports Anthony's being here. He has never threatened anyone in the school and his midterm evaluations are positive. I succeeded in arranging for him to enter the transitional living program, but on the day he was supposed to check in I was called to a meeting with the executive director and two staff from the social services department.

Sitting in front of what I call the executive director's power desk (it's about 8 feet by 5 feet), I am informed that Anthony is "too volatile and psychopathic" and a threat to the other participants. His pending attempted murder charges are brought up to prove their case. I am told that he was once arrested for assaulting Ana. I try to take this all in with an open mind, but it is difficult. I later talked with Ana's parents, who give a different story. They feel Ana is to blame for Anthony's outbursts. They are also concerned that she is not taking good care of her daughter. At subsequent meetings with the social services staff, I feel awkward. I have become an unwilling intermediary between the families, Anthony, Ana, and the agency. I want to advocate for Anthony. I try to stand my ground, looking for what I hope will be best for him and for Ana and their child.

Anthony is a complicated young man with a history of violence, yet no one wants to ask or seems the least interested in why he was selected to enter the high school or his record here. Not only has he been violence-free, he is doing his work and causing no trouble. He is not the only student who is attending or has attended this school who has a history of violence or is up on murder charges or has spent time in jail. The social services department has a different view of how to work with gang members. They take a "say no to gangs" approach. We don't advocate for gangs, but we respect each student for who he or she is and the life experiences students bring with them. I argued hard for Anthony. They agreed to withhold judgment until the following week.

Three days later, Anthony and Arturo exchanged punches in the student lounge. Arturo is from a rival gang and admits he threw the first blow. I've got to admit I'm starting to feel that Anthony attracts trouble. His rage seems to bubble over at the most inappropriate times. I pulled them into Patrice's office and tried to get them to talk. We set ground rules that included letting each talk without interruption. Anthony asked if they could speak alone. I reluctantly agreed, but told them I would be back in 10 minutes. I waited outside the door. When I reentered, they shook hands and agreed to explain to the next school assembly what had happened and to guarantee that it won't happen again under threat that if it does they would lose the chance of ever returning to school.

I didn't tell social services about the altercation. Anthony was accepted into their program and did well for about 2 months. Two weeks before Christmas break he was arrested for allegedly threatening a police officer. He said the police set him up. Stopped on the street, he was told they would press charges if he didn't get them a gun. Anthony went to a prearranged meeting site, leaving a gun he purchased on the street a half block away in the bushes. When he arrived, two carloads of police jumped out, pinned him to the ground, handcuffed and frisked him. They didn't find a gun. He said they slapped him around, charged him with assaulting a police officer, then dropped the charges when he appeared in court.

In the interim, Anthony was kicked out of the transitional living program because a staff member found the gun in his possession. Anthony explained that this was the gun he had obtained to placate the police. When he came back after posting bail, he told them he wanted it back. He came to see me up in my office. "I won't be coming back to school. I've got to get a job to pay for my lawyer and support my baby. Will you help me out with something?" He wanted me to get his gun back for him.

3

Rosa's Lost Money

I stayed home today to be with my youngest daughter, who has the flu. Patrice called about 10:00 A.M. She said Rosa, one of her advisees, left her purse on one of the couches in the student lounge and someone rifled it. She lost $240 and some food stamps. Patrice asked my opinion on what they should do. About the only thing I could come up with was a student assembly to talk about it and let them try to propose their own solution.

Elena called back at 10:30. They had an all-school assembly and now the students were meeting alone. She said the students expressed concern about the theft, but nothing happened about returning the money. Some of the teachers wanted to propose giving all the students paper on which they would anonymously write whatever they want. I didn't get the point of that idea, but our call ended when the students called the staff back to the lounge.

It's nice that they're calling for my opinion, but I don't feel as though I can be of much help from here. This is a tough one. I told Elena I think there needs to be some consequence if the money doesn't appear. The only idea I could think of was to suspend classes and count it as a one-day absence for all students, but I don't like that idea much. What I'm thinking is that we need to show the students we are prepared to take this seriously while maintaining the previous trust that has been built among students and teachers.

At 11:50, Elena called back to let me know the crisis had been resolved. The students asked the staff to do body searches. The teachers refused. The students then voted to search the student lounge and the lockers without staff present. About halfway through the search, staff returned because they thought the noise and confusion were getting out of hand. The students felt differently. It was decided they could continue the search. About 10 minutes later they found all the money and food stamps.

Another short assembly was held and the talk centered on their sadness as well as their anger about the breaking of trust. I was told they ended on a positive note with students and teachers feeling that, although trust was broken, they were able to pull together and work it out.

4

Claudio, Carmen, and Flora

This is the second time Claudio was pulled over by the police right in front of the school. It doesn't help that he's driving on a suspended license. Both uniformed cops are white. I walked up to the woman officer and tried to do one of those white-on-white routines. "I'm the principal of the high school, officer. Claudio is one of our students. What seems to be the problem?" While we talked, two other students, Carmen and Flora, got out of Claudio's car. The male officer put handcuffs on Claudio and pushed him into the back seat of the squad car.

"Your boy's got a big problem," the female officer tells me. "We found a bag of marijuana on the front seat, but we can't get back into the car." Carmen and Flora locked the doors and Claudio left his keys in the ignition. The woman cop said they needed to go get a "slim jim." They took off with Claudio.

Patrice and I talked with Carmen and Flora. They told us there was no marijuana in the car and that they weren't high. I wasn't so sure about the not being high part, but I didn't pursue it because the police had returned. As Claudio sat in the back seat of the police car, the male cop pried the door open with the slim jim and I continued my conversation with the woman cop.

"You let gangbangers in your school?" she asks me. I tried to be polite. "Claudio's a new student. We're a school that is open to everyone in the community. If there is a problem, we can talk with him here if you'll release him to my custody." She refused and walked back to Claudio's car.

I went into the school to talk with Patrice. I was sitting in her office when Carmen ran in and said the woman cop wanted to talk with me. "We're gonna give the kid a break," she tells me while placing in my hand a small bag of marijuana, rolling papers, and Claudio's car keys. As Claudio got out of the squad car, the male cop unlocked the handcuffs and gave him a hard shove on the back. Walking back to the school, Claudio headed over to a group of students. I said, "Hold on

Claudio, we need to talk." We went up to Patrice's office, where she was waiting with Carmen and Flora.

Patrice was most upset about the two women lying to her. "How am I supposed to believe you next time something happens?" she asked. "Flora, you've got a kid here in child care. What were you doing going out getting high at lunch?" Nearly in tears, Flora said, "We just went along for the ride. Claudio wanted to cop some weed and we smoked it with him, but we're not really that high." "It's not a question of degrees of being high," I told her. "We expect you to be straight all day at school."

This was the first time either Carmen or Flora has been in any real trouble, so we sent them back to class and Claudio off to talk with his adviser.

After school, I was sitting in my office doing paperwork when Paul came in. "The cops have stopped Claudio again out in front." I went out to the boulevard. Claudio was sitting in the back of another squad car. This time it was two plainclothes narcotics officers, one Mexican and one white. I took the offensive and told them who I was and that Claudio was a student at the school. As the white cop searched the trunk, his partner said that Claudio was driving without a registration and with a suspended license. Then he says, like they practiced this in the police training academy, "You know you got a gangbanger in your school?" Deja vú. I explained to him our gang-neutrality policy and he said we are too tolerant with these "gangsters." I felt like saying the police are the biggest gang in town as he and his partner strutted back to their car. I later learned they took Claudio down to the station house, held him for 6 hours, and then released him without charges.

5

Bobby and Willie

The two yellow school buses we'd rented for the day were late. We'd wanted to be on the road by 8:00 A.M. but didn't leave the school until 9:30. Off we headed for our spring outing and annual Cinco de Mayo celebration at a lake about 40 miles east of the city. It was warm and the sky was clear as we caravanned down the highway. As we approached the next to last exit, the lead bus pulled off and stopped in a small town mini-mall where we sat, looking out at three gas stations and two restaurants. The buses parked in tandem between the Amoco station and a Burger King. The drivers told us the fan belt on the lead bus had become a tattered piece of rubber.

While we waited, students, including some of the mothers with their children, went into the gas station and the Burger King to use the bathrooms. Fifteen minutes later the drivers announced they were ready to leave. As I walked across the Burger King parking lot to retrieve the last students, a young, scrawny-looking white guy in a white shirt and blue polyester slacks sneered at me and asked who was in charge of the kids in the buses. I tried to deflect his question and asked him if he needed help. "Two of those boys wrote gang symbols in my restroom." He wanted to call the police. I told him I would take a look. I didn't like his attitude, but I wanted to make sure it really was our students. I also wanted to appease him enough so he wouldn't call the police.

It only took a glance to see that it was Party Crew Boys graffiti. What a drag. The wrong place and the wrong time to be tagging some restaurant's men's room. I told the manager we'd get it cleaned up right away and he shouldn't worry. I walked back and called everyone out of the buses. I explained what happened. In as calm a voice as I could muster I said, "Either the people responsible need to come forward now or we're going to stay here and talk about this until we figure out together what we're going to do." I took a chance that they didn't want to lose their time at the lake. After an awkward silence, Willie and Bobby said they did it.

The three of us walked back to the Burger King. The manager had the cleaning supplies ready and they went to work. I noticed they had used indelible markers so I walked back across the parking lot and talked with the drivers. They agreed to take the students to the lake and send a bus back for us in 45 minutes.

It took Willie and Bobby about half an hour to clean the restroom walls and doors. I talked with the manager, some of that white-boy to white-boy kind of stuff, to try and keep him calm. He told me, "We're just starting to get gangs down here from the big city." I explained to him the difference between taggers and gang members and he seemed to loosen up. We got out of there okay, but I noticed the mirror in the restroom had also been scratched with tags the manager hadn't noticed. I kept my mouth shut as Willie, Bobby, and I went and sat on a thin piece of grass next to the parking lot to wait for the bus.

"Are you mad?" they asked me. "Mainly I'm disappointed," I told them. "This is an Aztlan Alternative trip and you're here representing the school. What kind of message does that send?" Willie pointed out that they cleaned it up. "People know who I am and what I do," he told me. I asked, "Why did you have to tag here?" "It's what I do," Bobby threw back at me. Then he said Willie didn't do any of the tagging. He was just trying to back up his homeboy.

I didn't want to put the two of them on the spot, but I knew that the tag on the mirror wasn't Bobby's. I said I didn't want them to snitch. "Just tell the student who did it that I want to talk with him. This is a serious violation of school policy and he could face being asked to leave school if we find out on our own."

The bus arrived. When we got to the picnic, all the staff, except Irma and Elena, were upset that Willie and Bobby were there. It was proposed that they sit in the bus during the entire picnic. I found that idea humiliating. Most staff wanted them kicked out of school. I asked for more of a process. Sylvia was particularly firm in her opinion and neither of us was willing to budge. I told Willie and Bobby, "Talk with teachers and students and hear what they have to say." One of the things I didn't think either understood was how strongly staff felt about how they had disrespected the school by tagging in the restaurant.

Recently I have become the fall guy in school in regard to discipline issues. It's not a role I want. It just sort of fell into my lap and seems to be working. I have tried to be an "un–vice principal," compared with the kind of administrator who traditionally takes on this role. I rely on discussion and agreed-upon consequences. But today I was feeling hung out to dry by most of the staff and it didn't put me in a good mood.

Irma came up to me a little while later and said she suspected Willie had been drinking. She asked if I had been near him since we got here. This was not something I wanted to deal with, but when we had our ceremonial circle before eating I stood next to Willie. He smelled like a distillery. Irma and I called Willie aside and told him we knew he had been drinking (which he copped to right away) and if any of the other staff find out, he'd have no chance of staying in school.

I needed a break. I went and got some tortillas, beans, and salad and sat at one of the picnic tables. Isabel strolled by and I said hello. I could tell something was up and I asked her to have a seat. I quickly realized she was wasted, probably from smoking marijuana in the woods. We have worked closely the past months on a collection of student writings she is editing. "Isabel, if any of the teachers see you like this you know you're going to be in big trouble, especially with graduation so close." She denied being high, but after I told her it was obvious, especially since "your eyes are half way back in her head," she admitted it was true. We sat quietly for a few minutes, then she began to talk.

"Sometimes I feel like giving up on school." Isabel works in a high crime neighborhood until 3:00 in the morning at a pizza restaurant set up like a currency exchange. It's take-out only. The employees are locked in behind bullet-proof glass and food is served through metal slots. Isabel tries to get to school on time, but she is perpetually tired. She is falling behind in the two math classes she needs for graduation. Her father keeps telling her she is wasting her time going to school. One of the reasons she works so much is to be away from him and out of her house. She doesn't want to hang on the streets and she wants some money, so she works, although she is only paid $2 an hour, under the table, tax free. "I spend most of my money on clothes and rings." She wears at least one on every finger. "I never got much when I was a kid and when I see something I like, I can't help myself. I've just got to get it." I tried to be encouraging, but I didn't have much to offer other than a sympathetic ear.

On the whole, the picnic was a success. We had a good turnout of students and the weather was great. Six mothers brought their children and most people seemed to be having a really good time. I played volleyball and hiked in the woods, even though I was getting the cold shoulder from most staff because of Bobby and Willie.

After arriving back at school, I talked with Elena and Sylvia. Sylvia is still mad and wants Willie and Bobby kicked out. I again argued for more of a process (although I sense the majority of staff are going to want them suspended until September). I feel Willie and Bobby are different people and should be looked at individually, although I think they'll get the same verdict. We agreed they would be suspended Monday and Tuesday and be asked to be available to come to the staff meeting Tuesday afternoon.

Bobby confronted me on the stairs first thing Monday morning. He said it was "no big deal" to tag at the Burger King. "The teachers are blaming me for everything." I sent him to talk with Sylvia. She said he advocated hard for himself, telling her, "The teachers are not really being here for me." This is a hard one for Elena to swallow. She's done a lot to help him out, including meeting with Bobby and his girlfriend, getting him into the temporary housing program, and setting him up for counseling. Bobby says, "I'm a tagger. It's not something I can control."

Standing by the couches in the student lounge, I asked students what they thought we should do. They said we shouldn't drop Bobby from school. I asked, "If I invite Bobby to my house and he tags up the walls and then tells me I should expect that from him because he is a tagger, don't I have the right not to invite him back?" Reynaldo said Bobby does tag in their homes. They don't like it, but they don't say anything to him. This revelation brought a change in direction in our discussion. "Maybe you can teach him a lesson," they told me.

No students want Willie kicked out. Everyone knows he wasn't involved in doing the tagging although he was in the bathroom when it was done. For Willie, it's more of an accumulation of incidents, including being consistently late to school. I told him this morning, "As far as I know, Irma and I are still the only ones who know you were drinking at the picnic, so that won't be held against you. But you've got to make your own case."

As the two of us were walking out of the building, I commented that he must be hot wearing a long-sleeve shirt today. He pulled up his sleeve and showed me needle marks and a Band-Aid. I asked him if he wanted to talk about it. He hesitated, but said, "I got out of the hospital last night from overdosing Friday night on cocaine." He explained that he was out with "the guys" and they sent a couple of them off to get some acid. "They came back with cocaine that I didn't really want to do but I did it anyway." Later that night he started feeling sick. "When I got home my heart was racing and my shoulder and arm were feeling numb." He took a shower and drank some milk, thinking both would make him feel better, but he got worse. His sister talked about taking him to the hospital, but his brother-in-law said he shouldn't go because they'd "put him in rehab." Finally, it got so bad his sister rushed him to the emergency room at St. Regis Hospital. The doctors told him he either started to have a heart attack or had a mild one. He's young, so his body survived it.

"I'm really scared," Willie told me. "When I was in the kitchen I felt like I was dying. I didn't want to die like this." He said it made him think about what he has been doing. I wasn't sure this would be a turning point for Willie, but I did feel he was thinking about some of his choices. "Will I be able to stay in school?" he asked me. "Be honest and give it your best shot," I told him as he started to walk down the boulevard.

6

On Strike

Spring session was breezing along when we were called to an all-agency staff meeting at 3:30 on a Wednesday afternoon. Rumors had been flying all week. The board of directors had gotten wind of the fact that agency staff are not happy with their decision to grant Raul Pérez, the executive director, part-time status to finish his dissertation. We never see him. We also know they are still paying him his full salary, which irritated us even more. The board asked him if he had the support of the full staff and he told them he did. The board said he had a week to prove this was true. No one is sure what is happening.

The meeting took place in the high school's assembly room, the largest room in the building, located down in the basement. Raul took the floor, standing next to a board member. Raul gave a brief history of his vision for the agency and opened the floor for comment. I don't know what he expected to hear. Staff members began to speak.

Helena said she felt awkward having this kind of discussion here in front of Raul with a board member present and with all the other staff in the room. It *was* awkward. Adan, standing near the back wall, said, "Let's be honest with each other and say what we think about what's been happening." Marta said the part-time schedule doesn't work. "It sucks," added Rodolfo. "It's not personal, but mistakes have been made and opportunities missed by us not having a day-to-day executive director." The floodgates opened. Other staff talked about lack of trust and respect, questioning whether this trust could ever be rebuilt with Raul. The board member also came under scrutiny for agreeing to the part-time status. He didn't help his case when he said, "The executive director is the top dog and you are the little dogs. We want this to move forward so that the agency has a good top dog as its leader."

Raul told us that finishing school is his first priority. He wants to know what staff members think so he can make a decision about whether to stay on. This is the first sign that he is thinking about resigning. Almost all of the 40 people in the room spoke. In near-unanimous agreement, staff members spoke passionately about working here, how the agency has changed for the better the last couple of years, and how detrimental it is having a part-time director. To his credit, Raul didn't try to defend himself.

Alberto asked to speak. "Raul, you need to look inside yourself and hear what everyone is saying. The handwriting is on the wall. You should resign. We need to move forward." At 5:30, Raul announced his resignation.

It felt like an insurrection. What a day. A number of people used the phrase "staff-driven" to describe the kind of agency we are becoming. I'm uncertain what's going to happen next, but as Sylvia said in the meeting, "We're ready to leap." The amazing thing is we really believe, as we take the leap, we're going to land on our feet.

A DRAFT HAS BEGUN for Sylvia to become the new executive director. She's being diplomatic and advocating an open process. One of the questions being asked is: If there is a management team, why does the agency need an executive director to "lead"? It's sort of a rhetorical question because the funders want one and I'm quite sure the board will insist on the "top dog" they say they need. We'll see.

Tonight is the joint board and staff meeting to talk about Raul's resignation. In an earlier meeting, we agreed to focus on the importance of moving this process forward quickly with full staff participation. Unfortunately, we shot ourselves in the foot. Six board members were present. Our feelings of liberation became a forum for staff to air out grievances against supervisors and other agency personnel. Sylvia tried to speak and was told by the board to sit down because she is a member of the management team. No one backed her up. Two staff asked that an outside consultant be brought in while others wanted to save the money and rely on our own experience and expertise.

I left feeling disappointed. Sylvia was upset with the staff. I don't blame her either. She was disrespected. I later told the high school teachers that I think this process is going to go on for awhile. "We should focus our energies on our work, plug in when we can, but try and not get caught up in a board/staff battle."

THE CURRENT BOARD is comprised of six members, three married couples. They decided, without staff input, to appoint Oscar Lara, one of the three men and a former federal bureaucrat, as the interim executive director. Their expectation is that he will become the permanent director. Tall, well dressed in a stylish suit and tie, he is a Chicano who grew up in the community. He called us to an all-staff meeting. Standing in the center of the assembly room, he spoke of building a strong and viable community service agency. He wants to work with us and we agreed to give him our support. The honeymoon was short-lived.

It became clear almost immediately that Oscar did not want or value staff input. He looked at the fiscal records and determined that the child-care center for young mothers attending the high school was not paying for itself. This is no secret. It was our decision that it was worth subsidizing since the graduation rate for teen mothers skyrocketed after it was set up. In addition, the mothers' children receive quality child care. Oscar made a decision to shut it down, effective June 30. And he decided not to inform us. Since it's a small agency and there is a network of people who look out for each other, we found out.

Elena and I went in to speak with Oscar about the future of the child-care center and he said, "I cannot discuss this with you because it concerns internal policy. No decision had been made, but even if one had been, I could not discuss it with you." The child-care workers have already been given notice. We called a meeting with the young mothers and asked Oscar to attend and to tell us what is happening. The mothers were angry. They told him how important this child care is for them and their children. Oscar listened. He explained that the agency cannot support a child-care center that does not pay for itself. He turned the issue around and blamed the mothers, saying if they brought their children more regularly there would be no need to close it down. This angered the mothers even more. With tears in her eyes, Angela looked straight at Oscar and said, "I would not be in school without our child care and now you want to take that away from me and my daughter." Oscar finally relented, at least in words, and said the child-care center would stay, but the decision would be revisited at the beginning of the new fiscal year in July.

OSCAR AND SYLVIA clashed from his first day at the agency. He usurped the management team and installed himself as the unquestioned leader. What Sylvia called "flat" management became hierarchical. Decisions were made in secret and then conveyed to department heads. On a subjective level, the decision that most perturbed the high school staff was the purchase of a shredder for internal memos. Why not put that money toward the child-care center? Besides, what is Oscar trying to hide?

After Oscar had been on the job for 4 weeks, we found a document stuck in the computer network printer one morning. It turned out that Oscar had trouble getting the printer to work. He didn't realize his print job would resume once the network was rebooted. What we found was a confidential memo to Sylvia telling her she was to be terminated effective June 30. Our allegiance to Sylvia is strong. We confronted Oscar. He told us that this is an internal personnel matter. He refused to talk with us any further. We called an all-school meeting and requested Oscar's presence. He appeared, but stonewalled the discussion. After he left, we talked as a school. We all agreed that Sylvia's firing is unacceptable and wrote a set of demands. Oscar had to immediately rescind the firing of Sylvia and we insisted that he commit to keeping open the child-care center. Alberto and Elena went to Oscar's office. He refused to meet with them, still claiming that these are internal matters he is not obliged to discuss.

We called an all-agency staff meeting in the student lounge. All but three staff and the business office agreed to a half-day strike in support of Sylvia if Oscar does not meet with us and agree to keep Sylvia. The next morning we gathered and waited for Oscar. He arrived 15 minutes late and spoke to the agency staff. "I am the decision maker," he told us. He said he heard there could be a strike. "I expect all of us to be at our jobs this afternoon." He refused to answer any questions and left for his office. We talked, agreed to go ahead with the half-day strike, and called for another meeting later that afternoon to which we would invite people from the community.

At 3:00 I entered the student lounge to find it jammed with nearly 125 people, including representatives from nine other community agencies. We explained our situation and everyone agreed to support us. We voted to call for a full strike. We set up committees, including electing a negotiations group.

The following morning we attempted to talk with Oscar one more time at a meeting attended by agency staff, high school students, and four board members. The students were fired up. Angela spoke. "How can you shut down our child-care center and fire our director and friend, Sylvia?" Oscar responded. "This is an internal personnel matter. It would be a breech of confidentiality to disclose information concerning Sylvia's status." In front of everyone, Sylvia told him it was okay with her for him to address the issue. He still refused.

The students became angry. They tried to ask more questions as Oscar turned to leave the student lounge. Students looked at me and asked what to do. "Follow your hearts and do what you think is right," I told them. They surrounded Oscar in the hallway and wouldn't let him leave. One after another they passionately explained why they are in school and why they want him to relent. They never physically touched him or threatened him, although he said later he felt his life was in danger. He recounted one incident, which I witnessed, where Luís, a bulky, five-foot-nine gang member, said to him, "Before coming here, I hurt people on the street, but this school changed my life. It has to stay open." Oscar said he thought Luís was going to hit him.

Two board members, including the president, called me aside and asked why I could not control the students. I said, "The students are doing what they feel they have to do for the school. I not only agree with them, I will not tell them to stop." I offered to help negotiate a temporary settlement and went to talk with the students. They agreed to elect a small group to go into an adjacent room with Oscar and the board president to continue talking, but they would not agree to postponing the discussions to another time.

This meeting led to 10 hours of negotiations. The staff negotiating team joined two more board members in the discussions. They hammered out an agreement that included reinstating Sylvia, continuing the child-care program, and no retribution against staff. Everyone agreed to sign. Before putting his signature on the document, Oscar asked to make a phone call. Twenty minutes later he informed the negotiators he would not sign the accord.

Shortly after midnight, negotiations broke off. We officially started our strike. The board asked us to choose one representative from the staff as a negotiator to the board and their lawyers. We unanimously said no. We elected a new negotiating team representing all parts of the agency. The board members left and no new talks were scheduled.

Wednesday rolled into Thursday by the time we left the building. When we arrived back later that morning, we held another meeting. Our meetings were based on the philosophy of participatory democracy. Everyone was allowed to speak and all decisions were made by a vote of the whole group. We met as a large group and then broke up into committees. We picketed the agency and wrote a flyer to be distributed in the community and to other agencies. Our minds were also on graduation, only 2 days away.

THE STALEMATE CONTINUED into Saturday as we arrived at the local park department fieldhouse to decorate and set up food tables. There was a pensive feeling in the air. We invited all the members of the board to the graduation ceremony, but none showed up. We decided not to make the strike a focus of the festivities. Not so with the board. We later found out they were meeting while the graduation was in progress. They voted to fire staff they considered to be the ringleaders, including Elena, me, and four others. On Sunday, when Paul tried to enter the building, he discovered that the board hired a team of armed security guards and a locksmith to change the locks. Paul immediately called around and we met that evening on the boulevard in front of the building.

We decided to come to work Monday morning as if the agency were open. We were greeted by the armed security guards, three police cars parked on the sidewalk, and a sign on the front door stating that the agency was closed until further notice. A security guard at a side door had a short list of people, limited to the business office and management personnel, who were allowed to be in the building.

We called another staff, student, and community meeting attended by over 100 people. It was time to escalate. We set up a media committee. The board went to court and got an injunction against us, which we voted to ignore. Students held a separate meeting. They set up tents and a 24-hour camp on the boulevard lawn. More committees were formed to prepare food and support the campers. On Tuesday, students made picket signs and banners and held a three-mile march through the neighborhood.

We met constantly, always in the open in front of the school. Some of the meetings seemed chaotic, but we never wavered from the principle of participatory democracy. We received some favorable media coverage, mainly from the Spanish-language radio and television stations, and the board finally agreed to meet with our negotiating committee, who reported back to the whole group after every session. On Tuesday, we learned that a dozen staff, myself included, had received certified letters informing us of our official termination. We knew we needed to make some decisions. We didn't want our momentum to dissipate.

We put out word for everyone to come to a meeting that evening. We talked about the lack of progress and called for ideas and proposals on how to get through this impasse. Following 2 hours of discussion, it was decided to issue an ultimatum. By Friday, if there is no resolution, we will do whatever we have to do, including nonviolent civil disobedience, to take back the building. This is our building and our school. We know we can take it back and we are willing to get arrested to reclaim the high school.

This ultimatum had its greatest impact on a group of former board members who did not agree with the current board's decisions. They also did not want to see this situation escalate into a physical confrontation. They asked to meet with us. We told them they had to talk with the whole group. They agreed. The large-group meeting decided to elect two people to negotiate with them further as another avenue of possible resolution, although we made it clear we were still committed to taking back the building by Friday.

In the midst of these developments, the staff decided we needed to unionize. We called in a labor lawyer, who helped us set up a union petition. He also informed us that the current board president, unbeknownst to us, worked for a federally sponsored labor relations group. This inspired us to call on that group to support our strike, which infuriated the board.

I was one of the staff elected to meet with the former board members. Their group included one person who is technically still on the board. Their proposed strategy is to call a board meeting Thursday night, invite all present members, and vote to fill the five vacant slots. This will create a full board that will vote to support our demands and oust the present executive director. We met in the back room of the local library. It had the feeling of a high stakes card came. We told them we didn't have time for further negotiations. We support them in their efforts, but we are tired and angry. We are ready to take back the building if our demands are not met. We will be in the building one way or another by Friday. We took this back to the large-group meeting that night. There was little hope that this renegade board faction would be successful. We continued our plans for a Friday-morning building takeover.

Thursday night the renegades called their meeting in a side room of the agency, where we still had access. The current members were notified, but refused to appear, saying they feared for their lives. A new board was elected and, seemingly, the coup was successful. They came out to inform us, expecting jubilation. We responded by telling them that until we are in the building we do not consider this a victory. The renegade board returned to their room to talk. They voted to oust the executive director, appointing two interim co-directors. They went to the security guards and informed them they would no longer be needed. The guards refused to leave. The police were called in and the security company finally agreed to leave as long as they were paid. At almost exactly midnight Thursday, we entered the building. We decided to keep people inside all night so we could be assured reentrance.

The next morning, we found Oscar standing in front of the school with a group of local police and an injunction ordering us out and telling us we were trespassing. We said we would not give up the building—they could arrest us if they wanted to, but we would not leave. We called some of the new board members. Two came over and spoke with the police, who said they did not want to get involved in an internal labor dispute.

Was it possible we won? It sure looked like it. The new board reinstated all the fired employees, with back pay. We formally ended our strike with a community celebration Saturday night. The sweet smells of home-cooked food, live music, a makeshift children's carnival, and nearly 400 people filled the boulevard on this warm summer evening.

Remnants of the strike stayed with us the next few months. A legal battle ensued between the old board and the new, with Oscar winning 3 months' back pay. We felt exhausted, relieved, vilified, and triumphant. It was a hard-fought battle. The students were wonderful and every major decision took place in large democratic gatherings, reaffirming the principles and processes of the high school.

During the 2 weeks we slept, ate, and lived together trying to save the high school, it felt as though we lived in our own little city. It was quite a high. Little did we know that within 2 years another executive director would appear, more vicious and underhanded than Oscar, and succeed in destroying what we and the students had worked so hard to build.

Guidepost

Cesar, Alexis, Manuel, and Gabriela, all recent Latino college graduates who grew up in nearby neighborhoods, and Stuart, a white, openly gay public service volunteer, joined the staff this year. Sal, Maria, Edgar, and Irma had departed and the youthful energy and organizing experiences of the new teachers charged the air with excitement. What I didn't anticipate was the difficult and time-intensive learning curve that arose as we attempted to balance expectations and philosophies of new and returning staff.

The focal point of much of our discussion was our effort to create a Latino-centered curriculum. On the surface, the issues seemed straightforward and based in our commitment to a school steeped in culture, language, and a curriculum rooted in the "Latino experience." Ideological differences rose quickly as race, conflicting interpretations of Mexican and Chicano identities, and the role of whites tore at our foundations and unity. As the problem was compounded by the new teachers' lack of teaching experience or study of pedagogy and curriculum, it took the collective initiative of former and present students to call us to the carpet and to explain ourselves and involve them in the debates for the survival and growth of the school.

By mid-December, individual agendas seemed to be put aside as Stuart raised the bar of cooperation and helped rebuild staff cohesiveness through a noncontroversial project. We followed this up with a staff meeting in which we sought to air our differences in a spirit of trust. It was our hope that when we returned in January we would come renewed in our commitment to put students first and search for common ground among ourselves.

7

The Centrism Debate

Am I psyched or what? This is going to be a great year. Half the staff is new, including four recent state college graduates, all Latinos. The other new teacher is Stuart, a white, openly gay, public service volunteer. Among previous staff, Edgar resigned to work on some personal issues, Alberto took a 1-year unpaid sabbatical, Irma went off to make films, and it was mutually agreed that Maria and Jane would not return.

Manuel Rodríguez, Alexis Salazar, and Cesar Puentes are activists who volunteered last spring and participated with us in the strike. They bring with them a personal and political commitment to work in the community where they grew up. This is just what the school needs. Sylvia is less optimistic. She is concerned that their political agenda will supersede what is good for the school. I argue hard to hire all three. "We can't pass up this opportunity," I tell her. Sylvia is not sure.

Manuel, fair-skinned and usually dressed in baggy pants with his hat brim turned to the back on his head, has a degree in history and will take over Alberto's classes. Barely over 5 feet tall, with short, dark hair, Alexis will team with Paul to teach math. Cesar, a few inches taller than Alexis, has a certain cowboy look about him, as if he just got off the *ranchero*. He'll teach science. All three strongly self-identify as Mexican. We also welcomed back Andrea Llanos, another young, self-identified Mexican who grew up in a nearby neighborhood. She replaced Sal mid-year as our Spanish teacher.

Gabriela Rocha stands in contrast to the other new Latino teachers. She grew up nearby, but went off to a private college out of town. She strongly self-identifies as Chicana. What most impressed me during our interviews was her passion for reading and literature. She will co-teach the English core classes and, I hope, serve as a counterbalance and a push to Robert.

We started our discussions with a week of curricular group meetings, the establishment of a new teachers group, and extensive discussion about Latino-centrism. Little did I know my bubble of enthusiasm was about to break, although I didn't comprehend it until months later.

THE COMBINED Spanish and English language arts meeting was filled with talk about the politics of language and literacy. We asked the question, "What is powerful knowledge?" We talked about grades and evaluations in the language arts. Teachers admitted that there is a tendency to shoot for the mid-range in a class with students having lower skills losing out. We need to figure out a way to address all students within a multi-age, multilevel classroom.

Elena asked: "What are the cultural implications of our choices of what and how we teach? What is the impact of a student's first language on learning style?" She noted that when she first came here, English was taught to be used and Spanish was taught to be learned. Spanish was presented in a traditional Spanish I/Spanish II sequential format, while English had Literature, Speech, Writing, and Drama classes.

We agreed to set up core English and core Spanish-language arts classes. We developed five objectives (or areas of objectives to be further flushed out) for the language program: (1) increase reading skills and comprehension; (2) writing; (3) translation; (4) structure and grammar; and (5) oral expression.

The math/science curricular group stated that their main objective was the development of critical thinking skills and logical reasoning. They wanted to overcome the mental block many students have toward math and science. They talked about connecting science and math to "daily life" and teaching both test-taking and college prep skills, including information that is "not important, but they need to know to take ACT tests to get into college."

What began to come out in the subsequent discussions was the need to ask "why." Why learn math and science? Why do the math and science teachers love math and science? What motivates them to learn and teach it? Sylvia asked, "What are the politics of math and science?" She challenged teachers to develop a framework for understanding what, how, and why we do what we do.

In the social studies, Manuel proposed changing the direction of how history and political science have been taught to one with a sharp Mexican focus, without any reference to Chicanos or indigenous peoples. This prompted Sylvia to ask, "Why are we teaching what we are teaching? What does it mean to be Mexicans in the United States and what does this mean about our view of Mexico?" She argued for a framework that includes the issue and impact of colonialism. Andrea and Manuel noted, without further comment, that we have to be clear on our definitions of Latino-centric as it relates to social studies.

This discussion became a preview of larger and more intense debates about what it would mean to combine and implement a student-centered and a Latino-centric curriculum and pedagogy. As we begin this new school year, I see this discussion as key to giving us the kind of rudder or directional focus we need to congeal, modify, experiment with, and challenge our previous work and to implement new ideas. I have a gut feeling that this is right. I'm also feeling like a kite flying in a strong wind. What does this white guy have to say about or contribute to Latino-centrism? I feel both out of place and in place. I know we need to begin asking questions that can propel us forward. In this light, I presented a paper to help generate discussion. In searching for common ground, I wrote:

> It seems important to note that the African experience in the United States is shaped by the Middle Passage and slavery, whereas the Mexican experience, although impacted greatly by invasion, white supremacy, and colonialism, is different in the sense of a common land base and language and the close proximity and interactions of families and individuals across the border, as well as the fact that prior to 1846, the entire southwest of the United States was part of Mexico.

I was hoping to push debate so I asked questions. They included:

> Is there more than one Mexican identity? What are the common identities and experiences? What are the differences and how do they shape the Mexican identity reshaped in North American society? What does this mean for a centric curriculum and, more specifically, what does it mean for Aztlan Alternative High School? How does this impact our curriculum, our teaching methods, who teaches, how responsibility and accountability are determined and expressed, and what role students, parents, and the community have in shaping and determining direction and decisions? What values are intrinsically Mexican or Chicana/o? What are the specific ways of being that Mexican youth and Mexican culture bring into the school and classroom? What is the role of language? How is one's learning shaped and guided by their first and second languages and cultures?

The paper attempted to define some frameworks that would allow us to ask the kinds of questions appropriate for our school. Finding little research on Latino-centrism, I looked to Afrocentric pedagogy and invited Dr. Edwina Williams, a local professor, to do a staff in-service. The combination of a white male–written paper and a Black woman discussing the relationship between African and Latino-centric philosophies turned into ripe fodder for the young Mexican staff.

Dr. Williams began her presentation by stating that both Afrocentric and Latino-centric curricula are new areas of thought and practice. "There is not much research yet to evaluate where they are headed." She asked, "How do different peoples and cultures view teaching? The school experiences of students of color are impacted by the race of the teacher. African American teachers are representative to African American students as surrogate parents, counselors, and disciplinarians. How students think teachers view them also impacts on how well they do in the classroom."

She raised the idea of teachers as role models and what this means for the sense of possibility for students, particularly students of color. She asked, "What are the teaching strategies that relate to and from a teacher's culture and race?" Statistically, she presented a picture of an overwhelmingly white teaching force in the United States where, in 1991, 6.9% of teachers were African American, 3% Latino, 1.4% Asian, and .9% Native American. In urban areas, it is more than likely that students of color are going to have teachers who are white for the better part of their schooling.

Dr. Williams asked us: "What are your expectations of students? What is your relationship to the community in which the students live?" She posed a duality between "narrow teaching processes" and teachers "acting as social agents," a process that is much more than mastering a subject area. She argued for a "structured, yet eclectic classroom" and emphasized that the reality of students of color is "different" and that teachers must "utilize teaching methods that reflect the community, culture, and language" of the students in their classes. Students need to be involved in the "change process." She called on us to "foster themes of personal and collective responsibility."

Pinpointing similarities between Blacks and Latinos, Dr. Williams stated that research shows successful teachers of African American students instill a sense of purpose and an awareness of African Americans in society, prepare students to "effect change," use African culture (recognizing that this is often in opposition to school policies), and educate for intellectual, social, and emotional growth. Looking at a

Latino-centric curriculum, she asked, "What are the generalizations that are helpful and how do we ask the right questions, such as: How can an Afrocentric curriculum inform a Latino-centric curriculum? How many students at Aztlan Alternative have had Latino teachers and what was the impact on their lives? What of Latino culture and the Latino experience can be brought into and impact the classroom, school, and pedagogy? What are the economic, social, and political challenges facing Latino students and what does this mean for the curriculum?" Finally, she asked: "What is the purpose of an education for Latino students?"

She ended by encouraging us to document and write down our experiences and questions and "find the one or two or three things you agree on and work on those together." She encouraged us to be explicit, real, and honest with the students. "Ask questions. Talk with them." She asked, "What does it mean for a student to succeed within a Latino-centric curriculum?"

I was quite impressed with Dr. Williams's presentation. It was informative and raised important questions. Why was it met with silence? There was no response. We should be making use of Dr. Williams's expertise and getting at some of the hard questions. I looked at Manuel, who had raised the most doubts in previous discussions, and asked him what he thought.

Manuel seemed hesitant to speak. After a few moments he said, "Mexicans have to have their own experiences. I don't think we should be talking about Afrocentrism because our experience is different." Dr. Williams agreed with him on the need to have one's own experiences, but stated that it is important to look at the similarities. Manuel responded, "We can learn from each other's experiences, but the most important thing is your own experiences."

More silence until Andrea said that the problem is white teachers who cannot understand Mexican students. For the next half hour, Dr. Williams could have been invisible as some of the Latino staff took aim at the white teachers. I generally don't have a problem with targeting white teachers, but this one was like shooting ducks at an arcade. This is a group of young Latinos, all under the age of 24, with no prior teaching experience, giving what felt like a political polemic rather than a critique. It wasn't fair to them, but I started to tune out, feeling upset that they were dismissing Dr. Williams out of hand.

After the meeting, Manuel told me that Dr. Williams should not have been brought in as a speaker. What he didn't say, but I learned later, is that he, Andrea, Cesar, and Alexis felt it was wrong and racist of me to present the paper. In their eyes, there is no role for non-Mexicans in addressing these questions. That includes African Americans as well as whites. What didn't come out fully until later, although we'd begun to see signs of it, was their adamant exclusion of a Chicano or indigenous focus.

8

New Teachers' Meetings

I had what I thought was a great idea. Because we have so many new, inexperienced teachers, let's set up a new-teachers group. I proposed we meet to talk about the art and practice of teaching.

At our initial meeting, Andrea also joined us since the extent of her teaching experience is the last half-year as Sal's replacement. We began with everyone describing a positive or transformative learning experience in his or her life. Giving up high-paying jobs emerged as a theme in their decisions to work at Aztlan Alternative. Cesar and Alexis were both on track to become engineers. Cesar worked two summers for a major aerospace company and saw himself on the fast track before he obtained what he describes as a "Mexican consciousness." He changed his major to history. Alexis stayed in her engineering program, but decided she wanted to "give back to my community instead of exploiting it."

All of the new teachers expressed the need to learn some of the basics or protocols of teaching and working here. Over the next few weeks we talked about everything from paperwork to how to structure an alternative lesson plan.

One of our earliest discussions focused on how to prepare for teaching and how to assess and address the needs of students. Manuel asked, "How do we present material that doesn't fall back on ways we were traditionally taught?" We talked of the need to "hook" students into the materials. This requires thinking of ways to get students involved and varied activities in the classroom that can encourage students to help each other learn.

"How do we teach the basics?" We talked of the need to be explicit with students about what they know and don't know. Expect frustration. Look to other teachers for support and always believe that instruction can change and improve.

When asked their biggest worries and problems, they responded with four: (1) how to teach different levels of students; (2) how to break through math and science blocks; (3) how to build nontraditional relationships with students, not just based on friendships or a belief that young teachers are the same as the students; and (4) when they meet with resistance, how to work with "unmotivated" students.

At our in-service, Dr. Williams named patience as a key attribute in good teaching. Looking at the first couple of weeks of school, she suggested that the new teachers set parameters and define the role of the students and the teacher. "Be up front with them with your expectations." She suggested they take some time every couple of weeks to talk with students about what's working and what's not working in their classes.

We met after school the first day of classes. The new teachers looked exhausted. They kept saying how tired they were. And it's just the first day.

Around the third week of school, our discussions became dominated by the Latino-centric debate. There are obviously big differences, especially among the Latino staff. "It is important what we call ourselves," stated Manuel. "There's a difference if we call ourselves Mexican or Chicano." Manuel and Gabriela squared off. Manuel argued hard that Mexican is the proper term and must be used because of its political implications. Gabriela stressed that "people born here are not Mexicans in the same sense because we are impacted by life in the U.S." Andrea spoke fervently in favor of the term Mexican. You could cut the tension with a knife. I tried to diffuse the harsh feelings by stating that I thought the content and the process were most important for us at Aztlan Alternative, but this didn't do anything to further the discussion. Like bulls, horns were locked tight.

After the fifth week of classes, the new teachers decided they didn't want to meet anymore. Personal tensions and political differences stood in the way of fruitful discussion. I tried to make the point that we need to listen to each other and practice the art of compromise, but I was looked at like a fossil. I was suddenly feeling much older.

9

Teacher Talk and Culture

By mid-session I was feeling incredibly frustrated. There was so much energy bouncing around the building, most of it misplaced. Staff were beginning to divide into factions: the self-identified Mexican staff, the self-identified Chicana staff, the white staff, and Elena, Sylvia, and I as a fourth group. The lines weren't totally distinct, but there were clear demarcations. What baffled me was that there were individual teachers who barely spoke to each other. I had such high hopes when we started. What's going wrong?

I looked for some common ground and decided to be honest with the staff about how I was feeling. I presented curriculum as a forum we could utilize to help us communicate with each other. I wrote a letter to the staff:

To my mind, the essence of a school is its curriculum. I take curriculum here in its broadest sense: prepared, in-school, out-of-school, and hidden curriculum. What is worthwhile to know and learn? This may seem like a straightforward and easy question (and for traditional schooling it is because it is supplied by specialists), but to be lively, relevant, honest, and effective, curriculum must be constantly challenged, investigated, evaluated, reshaped, and practiced.

We urge the students to challenge the status quo. Yet, if some teachers maintain low academic standards, assign little homework, and, by logical extension, have low expectations of students (and of themselves?), what kind of status quo are we asking students to challenge? Is this more of a disservice when the alternative to traditional education sets students up to believe we are something we are not? Is having "good" relationships with students, being "one" with students, an acceptable substitute for the intellectual risks of stretching the definition of student/teacher relationships beyond the dichotomy of teacher/friend versus teacher as authority?

To be a teacher here requires participation and engagement. The essence of this process is accountability. To be accountable is to engage. Engagement doesn't guarantee accountability, but lack of engagement guarantees that this staff will once again change after this year. Through our diversity and differences we need to develop and maintain a unity of purpose, philosophy, and practice. No one is going to give it to us. What we have is the opportunity to develop it and do it right here.

I think it's time to put our cards on the table. We each need to engage this process of curriculum development, evaluation, and implementation more fully. I honestly believe this is the key ingredient missing at this moment in time. This kind of engagement is not easy and most schools (as well as most jobs) never allow much of our kind of democracy and responsibility. We have a unique situation. We have the choice of pushing the limits to achieve some new heights or sitting back and letting opportunity pass us by. Personally, I don't want this process to stagnate and I don't want to be part of a school whose goal and practice is maintenance. Stagnation is complacency. It can only mean slow death.

These challenges can be intensely fulfilling *if* they are engaged and internalized. We face the dilemma of asking more of the students than we ask of ourselves. We tell students one of our expectations is that they begin to take responsibility for their own learning. What an exciting concept! Students are intensely perceptive and they know when they are not being fully challenged or when a teacher is winging it. They may not know we are not communicating well with each other, but they do experience our inability to create the best learning environments possible.

When we're sliding by, we only reinforce students' feelings of wanting to do the least amount of work possible in order to earn credits. Morally, politically, and pedagogically, this is unconscionable. Where is the meaningful discussion of curricular issues? If students can talk with teachers about curriculum and not worry about hurting the teacher's feelings, what stops us from being honest with each other? It's a risk, but isn't it the kind of risk we should be about? If part of our core philosophy and practice is the development of a school and curriculum that transforms the individual and we are not ourselves grappling with these same issues, the students are fully justified in labeling us hypocrites.

Would this harsh and long-winded diatribe work? We took an in-service day and devoted the first 3 hours to issues in the letter. The discussion began with Manuel informing me that "many staff were offended by your tone." We tried to talk. Andrea asked, "What if students don't want to do a lot of work?" She added that she doesn't give much homework because of student resistance to doing it. Gabriela questioned whether this is capitulation and the sparks began to fly. Andrea said she thought Gabriela was being too idealistic and that she, Andrea, was now more "realistic" after having been here 6 months.

The discussion continued to heat up. Gabriela turned to Andrea and said, "I find a certain homogeneity in Latino literature and I think we need to present more than just a Latino experience." Manuel and Cesar took this to mean that having a "Mexican consciousness" is not important. "All you want, Gabriela, is a college preparatory program," shot back Cesar. "That is a disservice to the students. The only way our students can go to college and make it is with a Mexican consciousness. If we don't give them that, we are hurting more than helping." Gabriela sarcastically responded, "What other alternatives do you have in mind?" Cesar stood up from his chair. "That's bullshit, Gabriela." "Fine," said Gabriela, "we don't want the students to talk to each other like that, so why should you get away with talking this way to me?"

Cesar, Manuel, Andrea, and Alexis surrounded Gabriela's chair. She held her ground. Sylvia called on everyone to sit down. Gabriela complained about being "ganged up" on and asked, "Why did you need so much firepower to make your point?" Sylvia tried to give us some order. "We need to know students as individuals and help them prepare for different kinds of alternatives, including college."

We ended the discussion, but no one was happy. I think I underestimated the need to talk about specific issues teachers had on their minds. Trying to focus just on curriculum was a setup for failure. Looking back, I realize that the college preparatory discussion should have told me more, but I wasn't ready to hear it yet.

THE FOLLOWING WEEK, Sylvia called me into her office and asked what I thought about having an emergency staff meeting. I told her I'm all for it if she thinks it can help. She named three issues: (1) supervision, (2) staff relations, and (3) Latino-centrism. She would talk with other staff and see if we could end classes at the lunch break and meet at 1:00.

Sylvia proposed herself as facilitator. We began by going around the room, everyone having an opportunity to speak without having to respond to anyone else. Andrea went first. "When I left Monday's meeting, I was feeling frustrated. I am bothered by our nonresolution of issues. I'm now asking whether I want to be a teacher and if I want to continue teaching here." Alexis, who seldom spoke up in our large meetings, added, "I am not comfortable yet speaking much at staff meetings, but I'm taking in information." She didn't want to feel as though she had to say something.

Manuel named our biggest problem right now as lack of communication, particularly regarding supervision. "There isn't any trust and I don't feel comfortable saying certain things." He raised a question about what our "vision" is of alternative education and said he thinks our differing views on this question are a major barrier to making progress.

Robert said he was trying to "get into the right frame of mind" and was also concerned about the nonresolution of issues. He questioned who has the "right to make decisions." Without being specific, he said that "several decisions have not been made in an appropriate manner." Patrice spoke next. "Staying away from people is my best strategy right now. You have too high an expectation of me." She added that she was concerned about the "racial tone" that is permeating the staff. Paul questioned our decision-making processes among staff and between teachers and students. Elena felt "tension and resistance." She wanted us to find a way to say "real" things to each other. "These kinds of problems don't go away on their own." She wanted to know what staff mean when they talk about communication. "I'm keeping to myself, putting my main energies into my classes. It feels like there are other agendas going on. This is something I don't feel comfortable with."

Gabriela said that she has strong "feelings of discomfort." She questioned how the offices are set up and who hung out where. She wanted us to find "new ways to disagree." She was concerned that staff are sending different messages to the students and felt that students are not being encouraged to believe in themselves. "We don't all have to like each other, but we need to figure out how to be more honest." Stuart said he doesn't have much negative to say. He was positive about his experience here and didn't know "what's going on" that's creating all the tensions. He thought that we don't have consistent expectation levels with the students and for their futures. His biggest concern was "making sure I'm teaching the students something." Cesar's issue is "consistency," which he named as having "more of a cultural curriculum." He asked, "What do we want to accomplish with the students?"

Sylvia wanted us to "concretize" our discussion and engage the issues. She asked that staff define what they mean by privilege, unfairness, supervision, and the role of white staff. "The issue is about power. I don't believe anyone at Aztlan Alternative is overworked. This is not the issue. With the white staff, I believe they should play a different kind of role. Whites can be good allies. The problem is defining what a good ally is."

Robert answered Sylvia. "I need to be taught how to be a good ally." Manuel criticized Robert's "missionary attitude." When asked to be specific, Manuel said he felt an air of superiority coming from Robert when he described the students as "these kids." Cesar questioned whether having students go to college isn't part of the "missionary attitude." He repeated his belief that it is "unfair" to encourage a student to go college who doesn't go with a Mexican consciousness. "It is wrong to correlate going to college with high expectations."

I spoke and said, "Not since the first year I was here have racial politics been such an issue." I knew the words "racial politics" would be a red flag. I gave two examples: (1) the Latino-centric discussions becoming polarized between what is the "correct" identity of a Latino/Mexican/Chicano and (2) the ostracization of Elena and Gabriela by the self-defined Mexican staff because both identify as Chicana.

We took a break. When we returned we got into the issue of supervision. We started by going around the room again with each person having an opportunity to speak. Stuart started and said, "Mark is my supervisor and I have no problems with this." Robert said he wants "clarity" on supervision. He felt that I made decisions without the full input of the staff. Paul added, "I don't know who's responsible for what around here." Patrice gave a history of our "struggle to get a coordinator" and how she felt that staff want the "convenience and benefits" of having a coordinator, but don't want to be held accountable themselves. She thought that some staff have been disrespectful to me. She emphasized to the newer teachers, "You need to be here awhile to understand what's going on."

Elena asked for a definition of our structure. "Supervision obviously isn't working because things aren't getting done." She was the first to ask if supervision is a racial question because I am white. If so, she said, then "name your problems with it and your alternatives." Manuel responded. "I believe the issue of having a white person as coordinator and principal is the primary problem facing us."

Sylvia took the floor. "We're not a collective anymore. This discussion is ahistorical. The bottom line is trust has been broken." In response to Manuel, she said the issue of the coordinator is "fundamentally a political issue." She asked, "Do you want us to shut down until we resolve the issue of the coordinator and having white staff?" No one responded in the affirmative and the meeting ended.

OVERALL, I DIDN'T FEEL that the emergency staff meeting helped much. We all went around and said our issues, but not much was clarified, although a lot was put out on the table. It feels as though we are becoming more separated as a staff and it's impacting negatively on the school. I'm especially upset by what I view as the arrogance and dogmatism of the recent college graduates. Whether it is their intention or not, they have gone a long way toward distancing staff from each other. I'm feeling personally burned by them at the moment. Over Sylvia's apprehensions, I fought to have all of them in the school and it's becoming obvious to me that they have decided in their meetings outside of here that they need to take over this program. I don't have a lot of problems with their inserting themselves into this process and becoming the next leaders, but I do feel they are being disrespectful of other peoples' work. In pushing their political line and agenda, they're making no effort to learn from other teachers. They have effectively dismissed all the white staff and any Latino who isn't self-identified as Mexican.

I'm trying not to take this personally. I represent white authority no matter what my politics or past history. This should be an issue we talk about, but they're trying to limit the discussion to race. To me, the issue is one of accountability and these other issues, including race, factor in but are not the dominant problem. I understand they may not feel similarly, but the way they jumped on Gabriela was a definite sign we're dealing with a collective agenda and it is not being put out to us openly.

I'm not feeling I want to deal with much at the moment because there is so little support for anything Sylvia or Elena or I do here. The new Mexican-identified staff is playing it so they get it both ways—they can critique, but don't have to take responsibility. Their ideas are primarily ideological positions. They have very little teaching experience, but I've learned it is pointless to refer to this fact.

Later in the day I told Manuel I think that all of them need to think about how they view their roles here. "Is it as a political organizer?" I asked him. "Do you mainly see Aztlan Alternative as a recruitment center for your politics? I think you need to take more seriously the idea of being teachers and educators. Teaching is not something that can be done well as a sideline. It needs to be studied, practiced, talked about, and evaluated." I stopped because I felt I was lecturing.

Sylvia is encouraging me to look at this in the long term. "This scenario needs to play itself out more." I can agree, but as I told her, "I'm upset with myself as well." I keep wondering what I could be doing differently to help get us back on the right course.

How can we change this momentum? It finally took the students to help us see some light and give renewed hope to the high school.

10

The Students Respond

Every year something happens—usually unpredictably, like the strike—that creates a conflict or crisis that needs resolution. Remarkably, while calling out questions, it challenges us in new ways and brings the students and staff together.

As we prepared for afternoon classes, the teaching staff was asked to attend a meeting in the assembly room. We were met by this year's returning students and Hilda and Lisa, graduates from last year. They told us they met during lunch. They want to air some things and figure out a way for the teachers to work better together. I didn't know if this was going to work, but I loved their initiative.

They started with criticisms of me and Patrice. We were told we are making examples of some of the old students while being too easy on the new ones. Angela asked, "What is your problem?" Patrice answered, "I'm frustrated. The old students know what the rules are and you just flaunt them in front of us. Mark and I are the only ones who say anything because no one else wants to. Then you get mad at us."

I told the students, "I am also feeling frustrated, caught between a hard place and a rock. I'm sorry if I've accused anyone of something they didn't do. I'm feeling like Patrice. We get set up as the fall guys and the only ones who seem to care that we have rules. We're trying to do the best we can, but it means we're going to make mistakes."

David stood up and criticized Robert for "copping an attitude." Robert responded by saying, "That's probably true, but I'm tired of being the butt of your white-boy jokes." Some of the other students tried to downplay the white/Latino issue, but Sylvia said students know what's up when they make these kinds of jokes. "We've all heard them here. They're not new, but we hear a lot more this year." Leon added that Robert is his adviser and he doesn't feel as though Robert "understands what I've been through. He's always on my case for something."

Hilda stopped the discussion and said, "What's wrong with you teachers? We all know you're not getting along with each other. You got sticks up your ass or something?" Lisa said we need to talk about why we can't get along because the "differences between you are affecting the students. You should say what they are."

As a staff, we stood silent. Hilda demanded, "You're the principal, Mark. You say something." I felt on the spot and I didn't know how much I should get into. "We have worked hard to pull together a staff we really want here. We've found out it's not easy working together when you hardly know each other. In the past, there hasn't been much consistency. Now, we have good but inexperienced new teachers. We have differences and we haven't figured out a way of working them out."

Hilda stopped me and said, "We want to hear from the new teachers, especially Manuel, Cesar, Alexis, and Andrea. You're always off together by yourselves as a group." Manuel spoke first. He said he is glad to be here and he knows "I am not a good teacher yet. I need the students to tell me what to do in my classes." Andrea said she feels the same. She wants students to tell her what to do.

Sylvia interjected that she is uncomfortable having this discussion without the new students here. Lisa said they told them they could leave for the day. Angela suggested we stop and meet again tomorrow with everyone. Hilda asked me if I wanted to say anything else, so I made a last comment about how I wanted to put out a challenge to the students. "As teachers, we need to take teaching seriously and study it, talk it, and evaluate it. We have a mechanism here to do some of this, which is the curricular groups." I told the students we need them to ask us what we are doing about curriculum, what happens in these meetings, and "ask teachers to see their notes and course outlines." Sylvia added, "We should get together and talk about the curriculum as a whole school."

THE NEXT MORNING, we reconvened with the whole student body after first period. Anamarie and Martha chaired the discussion. They started by asking new students to speak their minds. Some of the young women who have been identified as gang members said that some students (including Anamarie and Martha) are giving them "weird" looks because they don't belong to their gang. Eva, another new student, raised a criticism of Angela for looking down on her because she's new to the city. It came out in the discussion that some students have been calling Eva and her friends *brazers,* making fun of them as being country folk straight off the *rancheros* in Mexico. Sylvia got upset and asked, "Why is it we can't even respect our own people without label-ing everyone?"

Patrice and I were again the target of criticism for not fairly enforc-ing the rules. Their main complaint is that we are letting students get away with too much. Old students asked why we didn't institute a two-week probation for new students and why we were not cracking down on students who come back from lunch high. We both said how hard it is to know who's high and we don't really want to come down hard on someone without proof. We said students usually know, but no one tells us. They said they are willing to say who's high if we do the disci-plining. Eloisa stood up and asked to speak. Small and soft-spoken, she told the assembly, "If getting high is so important to you that you have to get high at lunch, then you should leave the school." She sat down to rousing applause.

I also heard it from Rosa, who quoted me as saying in class that I just wanted to start the quarter over, a remark she took to mean that all the new students were messing up. I explained some of my frustra-tions and how I could have said something like that, but it wasn't just directed to students, it included staff as well.

Martha brought up the fact that some of the teachers have "copped attitudes toward the students." I figured this was a continuation of the complaints about Patrice and me when Anamarie said the teachers were Andrea and Cesar. Andrea responded that she did have one. She announced that she was thinking of leaving the school at the end of the year and going to graduate school. "I have realized I am not a good teacher and teaching is not what I want to be doing, so I'm thinking about getting out now and pursuing other directions in my life." With tears in her eyes, she added, "It is difficult for me to make this deci-sion. I know I have been hard on students."

Cesar was criticized for being too tough on students about their homework. Manuel came to his defense and asked students to look around the room. "Who here hasn't turned in assignments that were due? We need students to set a better standard." I got his point, but I felt he was being hypocritical. I turned to Manuel and asked if he minded if I used him as an example. He didn't really have much choice and I think he knew what I was going to say, so he said okay.

"We have teachers who also haven't done their work and are not prepared for classes. Manuel himself has not turned in lesson plans or his syllabi." He responded by saying he had them in his briefcase and started pulling them out. I said he was not the only one and I could name others. "We need to help each other and you should help Manuel. This is an important part of what it means to have a student-centered curriculum. Don't let teachers get away with being unprepared. Talk with teachers you think have attitudes and bring other teachers or students in if you feel it is necessary."

THAT AFTERNOON we had another staff meeting. Manuel proposed that we use this time for a self-criticism session. He volunteered to start, but Cesar led off instead. "I know I close myself up and don't reach out and ask for help when I need it. It is hard for me to ask others for help." Andrea said, "I've noticed a change in my personality and attitude. I have become more cynical." She doesn't prepare lesson plans and doesn't think she is a good teacher. She has lost her enthusiasm for teaching. This is a major reason she is seriously thinking about leaving for graduate school. Paul said he is lazy and is someone who has "a one-foot-in and one-foot-out feeling" because he wants to go back to school full-time next year.

Manuel said he has done almost nothing with his student advisee files and he is still inconsistent about being here on time in the morning. "Some days when I come in I feel lazy and don't do a whole lot. Like last Thursday when I was out most of the night and came in after only an hour or so of sleep. I didn't do much in class that day." He said he has not been honest with me about his paperwork because he doesn't feel like talking with me about his classes. He feels defensive about the social studies curriculum.

Elena's self-criticism is that she operates on her own and doesn't always communicate with others about what she is doing. Robert said he doesn't follow through on his ideas. "I get pouty with the staff when things don't go my way and this drives me back into myself." Patrice said she is not being consistent with the students and that she over-extends herself.

I followed Patrice. "I feel like I have mostly failed this year. I haven't been able to successfully articulate what I think about curriculum or implement a plan that could help us improve our teaching. The only time I've felt we came together around curriculum was the one meeting we brainstormed together about the science classes. I end up getting an attitude toward staff and then I give up asking people to do things if I feel it will be a hassle."

As we were about to end, Patrice asked for last thoughts and Manuel said he senses a greater amount of cynicism, especially from me. I told him, "I agree, although I don't think it dominates my work." He said it did. I tried to end on a positive note. "In terms of things like empathy and care, our politics and practice around identity and cultural issues, and a commitment to the community, I think this staff is strong. It is in the area of pedagogy and professionalism that I see our greatest weaknesses. If we could focus more on our strengths and the needs of the school, I really believe we can turn this thing around."

11

Loisa and Jacobo

As we walked out of the assembly today, Maria told me that one of the women students is being harassed by a male student and we need to do something about it. She brought over Loisa, who said that Jacobo has been following her around even after she repeatedly told him she didn't want to talk with him. "During lunch time today he grabbed me in front of the building and carried me around the corner," she explained, tears beginning to fall down her cheeks. She is frightened and doesn't feel safe in the school with him.

I went off to find Andrea and Manuel, Jacobo and Loisa's advisers. Manuel tracked down Jacobo and asked him to join us in his office. We were blunt with him. Jacobo is immediately suspended from school, although he has the right to petition to get back in. To emphasize the seriousness of the situation, I told him his actions were illegal. "If Loisa wanted to press charges, you're looking at up to 15 years in prison." Jacobo countered by saying he didn't intend anything bad to come from what he did. "I just wanted to talk with Loisa. She shouldn't take it the wrong way." He said he's trying to get his life together and now he's upset we're "kicking" him out of school.

Manuel and Andrea told Jacobo he shouldn't have done what he did, but I sensed they were looking for some kind of compromise. Although I felt strongly about the issue, I tried to support them, especially since Manuel is his adviser. Andrea proposed that Jacobo write a letter to Loisa explaining what he did. He could give it to her and she would see if Loisa wanted to read it. I emphasized that Jacobo's only possibility of coming back is contingent on Loisa's feeling physically and emotionally safe in school.

Sunday evening I got two calls at home, one from Andrea, the other from Patrice. Saturday night, at about 3:30 in the morning, two guys and a woman came to Loisa's house and smashed the windows in her father's car, the same car he picked her up in from school on Friday.

There had been a party at which it was said that Jacobo and some of his friends threatened to "get Loisa for what she did to Jacobo."

First thing Monday morning I met with Andrea and Manuel. What a mess. The factionalism among staff is playing a role in how we deal with Jacobo and Loisa. This strikes me as strange because it seems to be a clear-cut issue of sexual harassment. Andrea, Manual, Cesar, and Alexis are arguing that Jacobo should stay in school. Their rationale is that this will give us the opportunity to continue to work with him and it will be the best protection for Loisa.

At our next staff meeting, we learned that Jacobo did not write a letter to Loisa, and he has been telling students it is Loisa's fault he is not in school. "We need to make a decision about whether Jacobo can be back in school," Andrea told us. I thought we had already made this decision. She continued by telling us that Jacobo is seeing a counselor. Jacobo told her that this is the first place he has cared about. He wants to come back to classes. Sylvia responded, speaking directly to me, Andrea, and Manuel. "As a staff, you've fumbled this one. You should never have negotiated with Jacobo."

We agreed that we opened the door for misinterpretation by giving Jacobo the impression that if he wrote a letter he had the opportunity to return to school. Andrea reluctantly told us she learned that Jacobo has been calling Loisa at home and having others call her to try to convince her to back off on him. Most staff are also convinced that Jacobo participated in the car-window incident. I spoke. "I think we have to make it clear to Jacobo and the student body that he will not be returning anytime soon. His actions were not only wrong, but criminal." I was attacked for this last comment. Manuel argued that we can't rely on the police. "We need a better solution," he added.

Andrea proposed that Jacobo be allowed to come back to school. Manuel said, "If Jacobo isn't here, there's no way we can guarantee Loisa's safety." Andrea added, "The main thing has to be about Loisa and that's why Jacobo should be here." "I don't see the logic," I countered, "in having the man that assaulted the woman back in the same environment with the woman he assaulted." Patrice and Elena asked them to spell out how they think we can guarantee anything.

Manuel reiterated that "we should not expect any support from the police." Patrice responded by stating, "There is no guarantee, but even when the cops are abusive to the victims, it sometimes keeps the attacker away." Looking straight at Manuel, she told of her own experiences living with an abuser. "Jacobo is going to continue to pursue Loisa and probably do the same to other women. He needs help.

We have to protect Loisa by not allowing him in the school." Manuel pressed his case, restating, "We need some other kind of solution."

It was finally proposed that Andrea and Sylvia meet with Jacobo and his parents and inform them of the incident and why Jacobo will not be allowed back in school. We will also initiate a schoolwide education campaign around violence against women.

Later that night, Patrice called. There's a meeting called for 8:00 A.M. tomorrow. She was told that Andrea, Manuel, Cesar, and Alexis disagree with the decision about Jacobo's not being in school. They didn't argue against the final proposal because they felt "intimidated" by Sylvia. I was really upset when I hung up the phone. I don't get it. Why are they are taking a stand in support of Jacobo and why are they targeting Sylvia?

The morning meeting didn't happen, but Andrea told me that there would be a staff meeting during lunch. Sylvia refused to attend. I walked in a few minutes late and asked for a recap. They were re-opening the discussion about Jacobo. A counter-proposal was on the table: Jacobo stays in school as the best protection for Loisa. This will give us the opportunity to continue working with him. Robert asked why we were talking about this issue again. Andrea said she felt intimidated in the earlier discussions, especially by me and Sylvia. Manuel added, "We've talked and feel that everyone on the staff is being defensive." I left the room so I wouldn't say something I'd regret later. I walked downstairs. As I passed Sylvia's office, she called out to me. "Loisa now wants to press charges against Jacobo. How do you think the staff will feel about this?"

Back upstairs in the library, the discussion focused on process. Patrice said, "We talk about how good it is of Loisa to speak up, but then we just leave her hanging." Manuel thought we have to look at the "bigger" issues. "Noncollusion with the state is something we have to make clear to the students. We don't want to be collaborators with the police."

This got me going. "What are we talking about here? The woman gets congratulated for speaking out and then the dialogue turns to the consequences on the man. Good intentions aside, the real scenario is that the crime was not the abuse, but the speaking out about it. We end up talking about how Jacobo's intentions weren't to harm Loisa and how he's going to suffer if we don't bring him back. Loisa is the one who ends up getting silenced. Where's our responsibility? What it feels like is we're giving this loud message to all the other women and men in the school that sexual assault is really not all that serious. If a white teacher made a racist remark about Mexicans and justified it by saying their intention wasn't to be racist, would we let it pass? Why, when a male student assaults a female student, have we spent so much time justifying his actions? And then we feel sorry for him? And think the best way to protect Loisa is to bring her attacker back into the school where she has to face him in class and in the hallways? I don't get it, everyone."

I should have stopped there, but I was on a roll. "And I really don't get this intimidation thing, especially since it is mainly directed at Sylvia, who has stood up for Loisa from the beginning. She's now branded as the intimidator and the bitch. What's getting defended here?"

I felt better for having gotten some things off my chest, but I don't know if it did any good. Afternoon classes were ready to begin, so we had to stop talking. Sylvia didn't return until our final staff meeting of the session. And Jacobo seemed to just disappear and his name wasn't brought up again. Loisa stayed in school and graduated, with her young daughter by her side, nearly 2 years later.

12

Personal Thoughts

I feel like I have been riding a roller coaster since we started in September. I had such high expectations and I have allowed myself to be blindsided over and over. I never expected this kind of resistance from the new staff. I've learned a lot. I know now not to use the word *experience*. As Manuel said to me, "We have experience too, it's just different from yours." "True," I told him, "but becoming a teacher is not necessarily the same as being a political activist." Occasionally, I'd call them kids and make a really stupid comment like "I've got a son older than you." Manuel would then spend the next week calling me "boss," which he knows irritates me.

As we were preparing for our end-of-session staff evaluation meeting, I said to Sylvia, "It feels like we have three alternatives: One, we keep struggling within the terms that have been set, although this has proven not to work; two, we back off and give it more time, but ethically I don't feel this is a good thing to do and I'm worried about the negative impact on the students; or three, we take the offensive and keep pushing issues out, but do it more in a Mohammed Ali type of 'float like a butterfly, sting like a bee' approach." She's ready to push.

A few weeks ago, Stuart's theater class performed lip syncs at the assembly to great applause from the other students. Stuart then proposed that the teachers secretly prepare some routines and present them to the final assembly before break as a surprise for the students. It gave us something noncontroversial to work on and the students went crazy. I said to Elena, "Isn't it ironic that a drag show set up by a blond, male queen is the first thing to bring all of us together?"

As I walked up the black metal stairs to the library, I thought about how the staff divisions and tensions have taken their toll on me. I feel distanced from staff. I put a lot of energy into the new staff and I'm feeling there's little coming back. I feel that just my presence serves as a validation of their oppositional strategy toward me and the school. I can't help but fret over how easy it is to be oppositional and how much harder it is to really throw yourself into a project and take your chances.

I'm trying to think of the best ways I can help the school right now. What I'm mainly feeling is that I need to focus more in the classroom. Personally, I need this and I want to set more of an example by doing curriculum and not just talking about it. I've been frustrated by the new staff's lack of interest in talking about curricular practice. It's little consolation that they don't seem to be talking with each other about curriculum either.

It's probably good that I'm in a contemplative mood. I am worried that some of the more subjective sides of our work are falling apart. One of the strengths of the last 2 years was a kind of centralist approach to resolving "discipline" problems. Students came to recognize that Patrice and I would be standing on the stairs or calling their homes when they come in late. Or, knowing there was a problem, we would be there to confront it. It helps students feel that the school is a safe place and free from outside or inside intimidation. This is now being challenged solely on the basis that we are white.

So, where am I? Elena, Sylvia, and Patrice say I should assert myself more and not be so easy on the new staff. Although I'm not completely comfortable with that approach, I do think I need to "impose" more curricular demands on the teachers. In my mind, what I want to be able to set up is some mechanism that helps unleash them to explore their classrooms and improve their teaching. The structural models I've set up have failed and I feel bad about this. I'm still uncertain of the reasons for the failure, but I guess to my credit I'm at least recognizing the need for change.

13

The End of a Long Four Months

Students are gone, grades are in. There's a light snow covering the boulevard as we settle in to wrap up our first months together. I propose that we go all around the room and talk about what we're feeling and then try to lay out some parameters for when we return from the holiday break.

Gabriela took the floor and spoke to the need to create an atmosphere where we can "be honest and raise things to people directly and individually." She was most upset that some teachers are talking about other teachers in their classrooms. "Personal shit should stay out of classes. I want to deal with people straight up. We should not have one standard for ourselves and a different one for students." She made the comment that some of what was going down reminded her of being back in college and "how white students acted."

Robert was quick to jump in. "Don't bring race into it." But no one else responded. Stuart said, "Until the lip sync, I'd been feeling like I don't want to come here in the morning." He asked us to search for a way to rebuild trust between ourselves. "We need to come directly to each other with our problems and talk and set an example for the students. My classes have been good, but I feel like I have lowered my standards for the students."

The room filled with an awkward silence. Paul spoke and said he thinks things are ending up "okay." He wanted us to "figure out ways to help the students get to know each other" when we start classes in January. Cesar added, "We need to set the tone in the first weeks. The last 2 weeks have been positive. Let's carry it on."

Elena was frustrated about our curriculum. "We didn't accomplish much of what we set out to, like integrating subject areas and developing activities. I am troubled by this." Robert thought students "lost their leadership from last year" and this contributed to the school's problems. "I feel frustrated because of the low standards we have for ourselves and for challenging the students."

Alexis said, in looking back, "I had many uncertainties about teaching and advising when I started. It was a lot harder than I expected. I made a mistake in waiting for people to step up and guide me." This led to her feeling unprepared for classes. "I know I can step up and be more vocal."

Manuel began by saying he was trying to learn from this session. "I feel there is a lack of trust among staff. Different alliances and cliques have formed." He admitted his classes were "very traditional." He wanted the social studies program to change and said he had been "irresponsible" in not being better prepared. "I know some staff think I'm antiwhite or too easy on the gang members or too easy on the tardies, but I never heard it directly from people. I want to hear these things from staff before I hear it someplace else."

"I appreciate Alexis and Manuel being honest about their mistakes," Andrea said as she leaned forward in her chair. "It helps me be more honest. I feel I took two steps backward at the beginning of the school year. I was too forceful." She was not as "optimistic" as some staff about school getting better. "I don't want to come back in the spring if things don't change."

Patrice began by referring to a party she attended last weekend with Paul and Robert. "I was bombed, but I really felt like staff was there for me. I don't feel like this at work. People aren't here for me." She felt a lot of anger and didn't know where to express it. "My job keeps changing and the rules keep changing." She questioned where the standards are in "making decisions." She turned to me and said she felt "very hurt" that I "gave up this session." She added, "Mark, you need to be more forceful and reach out more."

Sylvia was the last to speak. She walked to the blackboard on the wall next to my office. "I purposely waited until everyone else spoke." In an emotional tone bordering between anger and tears, she laid out her "report card" for staff. She began with retention and enrollment. "We started with the largest enrollment ever and ended with the smallest in over 2 years." She asked us to grade ourselves on how we did individually and collectively.

She went on to discuss accountability to the school's funding sources. "How many of us know beyond our own responsibilities what other staff are doing or who funds the high school and what the requirements are and what kind of files need to be completed?"

After each area, she said, "Give yourselves a grade." She went though time management, self-discipline, productivity, curriculum evaluation, staff relations, adviser/advisee relationships and responsibilities, building maintenance, and community relations. She was harsh, but in my mind not overly negative (which she said later was one of her concerns going into the meeting).

Looking around the room, she asked, "Where did you get this false sense of entitlement in the high school? There is a pervasive atmosphere of thinking only about your own things and not about anything else. Relationships with parents are very last minute, when they happen at all. Mailings don't even go out until a day or two before parent meetings."

Speaking directly to some of the new staff, Sylvia ended by saying, "I feel little support from you, *comaradas*. We should be championing academic freedom in the high school. We have more agreements than disagreements. I want everyone to step up a notch. Everything we do is interrelated. We need to look at the whole program. It is wrong to say it is our high school. This high school belongs to the community. That's who we are accountable to."

After Sylvia walked through the door and down the stairs, we sat around the tables gazing blankly at each other. A strange, mystical feeling seemed to engulf us. Four hours earlier, tension had filled the room from wall to wall. Now, we looked exhausted, drained from the meeting as well as the past 4 months. Yet it almost felt like a collective out-of-body experience as we quietly said good-bye, knowing we hadn't resolved our differences, but feeling that 2 weeks away from each other might prove necessary in rebuilding trust and support.

Guidepost

Like a sunrise on a cloudy day, wisps of positive change began to appear throughout the school. I spoke openly with some of the new teachers about our political differences and their view that I shouldn't be principal because I am white. Buoyed by other staff and students, I created a student research class that transformed itself into an independent, student-led evaluation committee that met with students and teachers and presented their findings to the whole staff.

With our differences more out in the open and the students organized as a collective and representative voice, we were now able to focus more on curriculum and teaching. Classes became more energized and it seemed that we finally settled into a routine that worked for everyone.

I still found myself at the center of controversy during the second half of the year, but the issues were directed less to race and politics than to student concerns, democracy within the school, and a renewed focus among teachers to create challenging lessons and projects. We began to look more to our strengths as teachers than to our ideological differences. During this time I began to think of our development as a birthing process. With possibly a mix of staff complacency and a desire to ride with our revitalized unity, the school year culminated like an actual birth, ending with both a major crisis and the serenity and joy of graduation.

14

Signs of Change

Manuel and Cesar facilitated the first assembly of the new session. Last year it was left up to me by default. At the beginning of the school year, they were all over me for not being democratic and now they find themselves in a similar hot seat. Their approach, which students have openly criticized, is impositional. For example, the murals in the student lounge are an eclectic potpourri of student themes and styles. The Mexican-identified teachers branded them "not political and cultural enough." They announced a time to paint them over as a first step to creating new ones. They were met with a tepid response and no volunteers.

Later in the day, I met with Patrice, Manuel, and his advisee, Roberto, who always comes late to school. Manuel has tried to rely on his friendship with Roberto and the fact they are from the same neighborhood. The down side is that he has done this to the exclusion of Patrice, who worked with him last year. The good news is that Manuel initiated this meeting and he was the toughest of the three of us. He told Roberto that if he can't get here on time he should stay home for the day and when he's here he has to do work. We'll see how much he carries through, but he didn't even come close to talking like this last fall.

A LITTLE OF my own personal spark is starting to come back. Some of it has to do with a different attitude coming from the new staff. It manifests itself in a more respectful approach to the school and the other teachers. I imagine most if not all the underlying issues are still there, but since I always like to look for the positive, it does seem we're moving in a good direction.

IT IS SO COLD we closed the school for 2 days. The high yesterday reached minus 11 degrees. It feels as if we're a bunch of dead cows hanging in a meat freezer. Only Paul, Sylvia, and I showed up at school, but the heat was on and it gave us a chance to catch up on some paperwork.

I got a call from Patrice. She asked me if I was going to the political program Manuel, Cesar, Andrea, and Alexis have planned for Saturday night. I didn't even know about it, which is okay, but there is an air of secrecy that is disturbing. They asked Patrice to give them all the students' parents' names and phone numbers to invite them to their forum on Chiapas, which just exploded in insurrection in southern Mexico. I also learned that they have a protest planned for next Wednesday at noon at the Mexican consulate. Let's hope they bring it up at the staff meeting.

I told Patrice to call Sylvia to get her opinion on giving out the names and phone numbers. Sylvia said that if they wanted the numbers they'd have to go through her, short of a discussion by the whole staff. Once again we are forced into an awkward "authority" cycle. Patrice called me back and said she'd take care of it. Fifteen minutes later she called again. "They aren't happy about this decision. Andrea told me I should give them the information because you and Sylvia don't have to find out." This pushed me back over the edge. Tensions have lessened and they seemed to be keeping more of their business outside of school, but maybe we aren't making as much progress as I thought.

The Tuesday staff meeting had a strange quality to it. I waited for someone to bring up the protest. Manuel skirted the issue by saying he is concerned about "some students" feeling there will be repercussions if "they do something in support" of the Chiapas rebellion. "What students are you talking about?" I asked. He couldn't or wouldn't name anyone. I said, "Our school philosophy is that everyone has the right to express opinions."

Cesar said he wants to call a special assembly in the morning about a Chiapas protest tomorrow at noon. I asked why we couldn't have done this last week. He told me they just found out about it, which I knew was not true. I finally said, "What's going on? I don't understand the need for all the secrecy." There was no response.

After the meeting, I talked with Manuel and told him I thought their group had violated the trust of the staff by not being honest with us about the protest. "I get the feeling you think the school is yours. You meet outside of here as a collective and you have a strategy for taking the school over. Why can't we work together? I know you hate me talking about inexperience, but you are politically inexperienced too and it is showing." Manuel didn't take kindly to my rebuke. "We have our own experience," he reminded me. "We never lost a struggle at the university. We know how to win."

We started the next day with an assembly in the student lounge because it was still too cold to meet downstairs in the assembly room. Manuel told the students that attendance at the protest is voluntary, which I took as a positive sign. He and Cesar went on to say that students had to "be serious." They made it clear that everyone will know who stays back and who wasn't "serious about being Mexican and supporting their brothers and sisters in Mexico and Chiapas." What a gut check.

At 11:00 we broke from class and milled around for about half an hour waiting for the bus. We got to the demonstration 10 minutes early, the first ones to arrive. We started picketing, about 75 people from Aztlan Alternative plus a few leftists from political groups. Over the next half hour maybe 20 other Latinos from area colleges came by and around 12:40, 15 students from another alternative school showed up.

I'm having mixed feelings as I walk the oblong picket line with the students. Am I just an old white male leftist dinosaur? Why do I feel like I've been here too many times before? The whole protest seems to have come out of an activist protest formula manual. The demonstration "security" is all male, the "speeches" are steeped in rhetoric, and the organizers (our group of teachers) keep huddling to talk, looking like some kind of anointed central committee. They also promised we'd be out of here no later than 12:45 and it's already past 1:00 and freezing cold.

When we finally arrived back at school it was 1:45. Students gathered in the lounge and said they didn't want to go to class. Elena and I were the only teachers around and I told the students we really wanted to have the last class of the day (which we'd agreed on at the staff meeting). Resistance was heated. I went looking for Manuel, Cesar, Andrea, and Alexis to help out. I found only Manuel and Cesar, who were in a meeting evaluating the protest. I told them they were needed in the student lounge. Manuel came upstairs and told the students they should be in class and then he and Cesar went back to their meeting. Not more than 5 minutes later, students called an emergency assembly to talk about why they had to be in class. Again, Elena and I were the only teachers available, so I told the students they were free to go.

This has been an exhausting day. I feel pulled in conflicting directions. I'm particularly concerned about how politics seems to be impinging negatively on our ability to grow as a school. Over the next couple of weeks I would seek out Manuel and Cesar, the leaders of their collective, to talk.

I ASKED MANUEL to join me in my office. I gave him the comfortable chair. We began by discussing the state of the school. I asked him what he envisioned for Aztlan Alternative in the upcoming months. He told me, "It's limited what we can do." "What do you mean?" I asked. "We can't do what we want to do here," he said without being specific. With a little more probing, he volunteered that "some" teachers shouldn't be here. "We have different conceptions of what alternative education is," he said. "But why not rely more on the staff cooperative?" I asked him. "Everyone's too cynical," he responded. "Except you?" I asked. "I'm not," he said. "We need to get rid of certain staff and have a different focus to the school, including changing the name. We should name it after Flores Magon."

I told Manuel that I think he and his group are being too stringent and dogmatic in their conception of what we can accomplish here. "Why don't you just set up your own school?" "That's what we've always wanted to do," he replied. I told him I thought they'd face similar problems. "But maybe it's something you have to see firsthand for yourselves." He agreed.

We went back over who is working here. I tried to break it down into where people stand in relationship to why they teach at this school. It came down to the Mexican-identified teachers, the faith-based white staff, and Elena, Sylvia, Gabriela, and me. Manuel kept saying "We need to do things differently," but he didn't want to share any new ideas with me. "Do you really want to know what others think, including me, or do you just want to implement what you think is best?" I went on to say that I respect their right to meet and talk outside the staff cooperative. "But, I don't believe having all of these outside discussions and then trying to implement something while consciously disregarding others' input is going to work." He didn't respond.

"I think you're being nearsighted, Manuel. One example is how all of you have related to me. We could work together and pool our knowledge and experience, but, for whatever reason, you don't want to. I've tried to make it clear, although I've failed in this regard, that I have a political commitment to help you out as much as possible, a pedagogical commitment to work with you as teachers, and a personal commitment between us as activists and organizers. I guess I have to realize that if you don't want this, I need to back off and make do as best as possible. Maybe it's taken me too long to realize this, but I'll stop pushing you as hard as I have." It was time for class. We agreed to talk later.

CESAR AND I sat down at one of the round tables in the library. "We need to talk more about the direction of the school," he told me. "What it's about and where it's headed." We kept to the safe topics until I asked about their collective and what ideas they had for the school. He denied that they meet or discuss the school. I got right to the point. "I don't think it's right or possible for someone to impose their political line on the school. It's different being activists on a college campus than working and organizing in an alternative institution in a community."

I told Cesar I thought they were making political judgments based only on their perspectives and interests. They are not listening to or respecting the people who have been working here, some for years. I asked him if he agreed with what Manuel has said about me and the other white teachers working here. He said he did. "I think the issue of a white director is the primary one and has to change." "What about Sylvia?" I asked. "You seem to have more political disagreements with her than me. Is it because I'm white or are there more substantive issues?"

"We came here to be in the community, to work with Mexican youth," Cesar told me. "And I was the one who encouraged you and fought in the staff to have all of you hired," I responded defensively. "We needed to make some drastic changes and we needed your political input and energy and leadership. You can be great role models for the students." He described their time here last spring during the strike as "checking out whether we felt we could work here."

I questioned Cesar about how they conceive of their role. "In my opinion," I told him, "it has to be more than as political organizers. Aztlan Alternative can't just be a recruitment center for your politics. One thing I'm looking for is that you take more seriously being teachers and educators. Teaching is not something that can be done well as a sideline. It needs to be studied and talked about and evaluated."

Cesar talked about implementing a Mexican-centric curriculum. "As a policy issue, the main question is what definition is given to it." I told him I thought the discussion had been too abstract. As we ended the school day, I said, "To tell you the truth, Cesar, I feel this is the year when a transition can take place with Aztlan Alternative. Your group can play a major role in this, but you have to want to see beyond your own organization and its political line. Whether I or any of the other whites stay on staff is a real issue, but it's got to come out of a process of discussion and practice."

I talked much more than I wanted, but I do feel Cesar is a respectful listener. The following week I got an opportunity to talk with Cesar and Manuel together.

BACK IN MY OFFICE, Manuel sat on the large windowsill overlooking the boulevard and Cesar brought a chair in from the library and sat by the door. They asked me why I stayed at Aztlan Alternative and why I want to work with them.

"My motivation is threefold," I said. "One is a political commitment to help you out as much as possible. In the face of what I've felt is resistance, I've pushed anyway. I don't know if that is a good idea or not. Second, I genuinely believe each of you can be a good teacher. With you Manuel, I feel you're trying to ride on your charisma in the classroom. Good politics doesn't automatically translate into good teaching. Learning to teach is a process. I think if you put more attention into preparing for your classes and evaluating your work, you can become an excellent teacher. But, it takes work. I thought I could help you out in this regard. For whatever reason, that hasn't worked between the two of us and I accept that. Third is a more personal reason, but something I also consider to be profoundly political. I believe in what we're doing here and I have high expectations for what the current teachers can accomplish."

Cesar and Manuel looked at each other and then back at me. I continued. "I know we have differences. But, you know, I think this is healthy. As far as our working relationship in the school, I will back off. As far as the political discussion we're having, from the beginning I have found it unfortunate that there is such a chasm between the group of you and myself. Maybe it's age, maybe it's race, maybe it's deeper political differences that I am not aware of. I don't know. It's probably a combination of factors, but I find it extremely unfortunate we haven't been able to build a political trust that allows for more open and forthright dialogue. At this point it seems more characterized by anger and frustration. Our political histories are different. I've tried to place myself back to when I was in my early 20s and how I felt. I think I understand the fervency and commitment of what you are trying to accomplish. I know I can't know or fully appreciate it as much now as I did then. Only time will tell if a political idea, line, or project will work. I have no hidden agenda. I'm trying to put my cards on the table with you, although I probably don't always do it in the most appropriate ways. But I don't believe I've been dishonest with you. If you think that is wrong, you should say."

In looking at what we can accomplish in the high school, I said, "My approach is to put everything into it as far as we can push it. I believe some of the barriers you are putting up are self-imposed. There is more latitude and freedom here than I think you want to acknowledge. It can be played out farther than you are giving it credit for. That isn't to say it's any kind of utopia, but to my mind the problem with self-imposed barriers is that they limit learning. I know you want to set up your own political project and school. But for now, what lessons can be learned from this school that can help guide that process? Again, to my mind, it is the combination of theoretical ideas and the practice of doing them that guides strategy. I guess for me, and this doesn't have to be true for you, they haven't yet been played out as far as they can go in the high school.

"My main criticism has been that a politics cannot be imposed carte blanche from a collective outside the high school. What may seem totally righteous to you isn't always perceived that way by others. I have never understood why you can't just put more things out to the staff. Even if an idea isn't accepted initially, I do believe correct ideas win out in the long run. People get won over when they see that something is right. The worst way to win a struggle is to impose it."

Was I talking too much again? Manuel finally said, "Our collective acknowledges that there's problems and we have a role to play in creating them. Our intentions are to work with the students, not necessarily build the school. We have lots of disagreements among ourselves. We're not this big bloc everyone thinks we are." I pointed out that we never see that in staff meetings. He gave an example of how he disagreed with Cesar and Andrea about a student. "Why didn't you say anything," I asked. "This is an example of how you are perceived as a unified bloc who never disagree with each other." Manuel asked what I thought could be done to make things better.

I told him it would be good if someone from their group spoke at the staff meeting about how they have contributed to some of the tensions and now resolve to help improve relations among teachers. I also think they should be more conciliatory around the Chicano-versus-Mexican identity discussion and take a different approach around the white-principal issue, at least until June. They agreed, but asked in return that I not pick on them so much, especially Manuel and his lack of curriculum paperwork. I reluctantly said okay, but I told him I would like to sit down and talk curriculum and see where we could help each other.

15

Jaime

The legal age to leave high school is 16, which is why the state requires our students be 16 years of age or older. For some reason, they believe that no one under that age ever leaves school. It is not unusual to get calls from mothers asking if we can take their 14- and 15-year-old children or to have students apply who have never attended high school. Occasionally, applicants lie about their age to get into the school.

Jaime looked to be about 13 years old. Slight of build, not much over 5 feet tall, he had an impish look with his dark hair pushed to one side of his head. During orientation, he was quiet and his mother told us he met the age requirement. To protect ourselves, we asked him to bring a birth certificate to his interview. I also talked with students who knew him from the neighborhood and they vouched for his age. During the interview, he told us he had attended high school for only 3 days. He said he was not in a gang, but had been threatened by gang members. He felt it prudent to quit while ahead.

We accepted Jaime, and I became his adviser, whereupon I got to know a different Jaime. We know prospective students are usually on their best behavior during the orientation and interview, but we're usually able to get at least a glimpse of their true personalities. Within days, Jaime went from shy introvert to loud extrovert. Students nicknamed him "Geraldo" after the talk-show host. Jaime had an opinion on anything and everything. I also realized, contrary to what he told us, that Jaime was in a gang not affiliated with any of the other gangs at school. This left him vulnerable, although he was safe as long as he kept his affiliation to himself.

The first sign of trouble came to my attention when Lanie called me aside and said Jaime was "fag-baiting" him in the halls. Lanie had asked him to stop, but Jaime persisted. I called Jaime up to my office. To protect Lanie, I told him a teacher overhead his remarks. I explained our policy about name-calling and homophobia. He told me, "But he *is* a fag." He said this is how he talks at home and I told him that this isn't his home. "Here, everyone has the right to be who they are and be safe and respected." He said that was okay with him, but I don't think he really agreed.

The very next day I got a call from the social services department in the rear of the building. They said Jaime had been working on their bathroom yesterday for his carpentry class. When he left, they noticed gang symbols written on the bathroom walls and one of the social workers was missing a $10 bill and his beeper from his jacket.

I found Jaime and told him we needed to talk. He didn't want to, but I insisted. I explained what I had been told and he denied everything, even though he is the only student associated with the tagged gang symbols. I said, "Whether you did it or not, it would be a nice gesture if you would volunteer to clean it up." He refused. I told him we were going to announce the theft of the beeper in the assembly and ask that it be anonymously returned. Jaime complained that he not only shouldn't have to clean up the room, "but, if someone leaves something out, it's fair game." "What if someone stole something of yours?" I asked him. "That's my fault," he explained. I tried taking a more serious tack and asked him if he ever worried about getting arrested and possibly going to prison. He said no because he's underage. "I do what I gotta do," he told me. "If someone gets in my way, that's their problem."

Jaime didn't show up for school the next 2 days so I called his house. His mother answered. "He was sick yesterday. He left at seven this morning and should be there." I told her he hadn't arrived. She hesitated. "Jaime didn't want you to know, but he told me he was threatened in the student lounge and he's afraid to come to school." He told her two guys said they would "blow him away."

I assured her that Jaime was safe in the school and that we insist on a policy of nonviolence and neutrality from all students. When there is a problem, we initiate discussions with everyone involved and try and reach a quick resolution. I politely tried to point out that Jaime was not an innocent kid. "My son is not in a gang," she said. This put me in a slightly awkward position. I've noticed that around his mother, Jaime is like Eddie Haskell was to Beaver's mom. I told her I would talk with him if he arrived at school.

Jaime showed up during second period. I called his mother to let her know, then met with Jaime. He recounted that five or six students confronted him in the student lounge and told him he wasn't welcome in the school. In addition to saying they would "blow him away," he said he was told he was not welcome here because of his gang affiliation. He went on to tell me again that he is not involved in gang activity and doesn't know why he would be hassled. He did admit he "hangs on the street" with gang members in his neighborhood. He said he was worried about going home on the bus because he has to wait at a bus stop that is in rival gang territory.

I told Jaime we would do what we could and he pushed me on what that meant. I said we'd watch more closely what was happening and talk with whoever needs to be talked with. He worried they would find out he talked with me because they also warned him not to tell anyone. There was something fishy about his story, although it was not inconceivable.

Later in the day I talked with Carl, who is in a gang loosely affiliated with Jaime's. Carl is a large manchild with a sweet personality and a volatile temper that got him in trouble on the street. He's trying hard to pull his life together and works at a restaurant over 50 hours a week while attending school. He got kicked out of his last school for throwing a chair at a teacher. I asked him if he would be willing to talk with Jaime. He agreed. I saw them talking together at lunch that day. Carl later told me he "schooled" Jaime on how to carry himself. "There shouldn't be any more problems."

Jaime didn't show up for school the next 2 days. On the following Monday I called his house. The phone was disconnected. Elena and I drove over to the building where he lived. We didn't have an apartment number and the family name was not on any of the mailboxes. We knocked on a door where it looked like someone was home. A woman with two small children opened the curtain and talked to us through the closed window. She said Jaime's family had moved out on Saturday. We never heard from him again.

16

Lucia

About half an hour after school let out, I sat in my office chair staring blankly out the window. I noticed Lucia walking across the boulevard with Jason and Rogelio. All three had gone off in Jason's car at lunch and had not returned. Our policy on cuts was a meeting with the adviser, an automatic one-day suspension, and a student-written statement on what happened and what kinds of consequences they think are appropriate.

I decided to greet them as they walked up the stairs. We met in the second-floor alcove where I was overwhelmed by the smell of alcohol. "What's up?" I asked. "You want the truth?" Lucia responded. "That would be nice," I answered.

Lucia confessed they had been drinking. "I know," I said. "How?" she asked. I laughed and said, "It's pretty obvious by the smell and how wasted you all look." "What's going to happen to us?" Jason asked. Rogelio and Jason are new students. I explained our policy and asked them what they thought would be an appropriate consequence. "Could we clean the building?" Jason offered. I told him I couldn't make that decision on my own. "You think about it over the weekend and talk with your advisers on Monday."

The two guys left while Lucia sat down on a chair in the student lounge. She said she had planned on coming back right after lunch "but I was too buzzed to drive my car." It didn't seem to register that she shouldn't have been drinking at lunch to begin with, but I told her I was glad she didn't try to drive while she was drunk. "I'm still pretty buzzed, but I drove here anyway."

I went and found Elena and we brought Lucia up to her office. It seemed clear that Lucia came back for a reason and she didn't want to leave. I told her if she was going to be here she had to stay away from other staff in the building because they would not understand why a drunk student was in the school.

Lucia started to talk about the father of her son, who is in jail. He's been there for nearly 2 years and is getting out next week. He wants to see her and her child and he's told her he wants the money he left behind, which she claims she knows nothing about. She's scared. Lucia has already legally signed over custody of her son to her parents, but she's afraid the father will challenge them in court. "I know I'm not the best mother, but I try," she told us. "He's a gang member and a drug dealer. I don't want nothing more to do with him. But he won't go away. He calls my parent's house from jail, but I never talk to him."

Elena and I listened. We didn't have any answers. The conversation seemed to sober Lucia. She told us she wanted to go outside for some fresh air. We didn't see her for 3 weeks. The father of her child did not get released. Lucia wants to come back to school. We argued her case at the staff meeting. They turned her down, but said she could petition to return next session.

17

Hitting Rock Bottom

My advisee group was talking in the library when Stuart walked in complaining about the cigarette smoke in his office. Gabriela's advisee group meets there daily. He had asked them to stop, but they refused. He wanted me to intervene. I walked across the hall and found Gabriela and five students. Everyone was smoking. The haze was so thick it was hard to breathe. They didn't even have the window open. I looked at Gabriela and said, "Everyone needs to put out their cigarettes. It's against school policy and a violation of the fire regulations. That's why we have the smoking room downstairs." The whole group looked right through me like I didn't exist.

Since they also had the radio on, maybe they didn't hear me. I told them again and Lena made a snide comment about how they don't have to listen to me. This is Gabriela's group and her office. Lena is one of those students who works at getting teachers irritated at her. I tried not to bite back at her comment. I asked Gabriela to talk with the students. She just laughed at what was going on and turned away. Lena said, "We can do whatever we want. Why are you picking on us?" I was getting really irritated. "The fire department could shut down this place if they knew this was going on and, besides, the students were the ones who voted on the smoking room. Why are you flaunting the rules?"

Lena shot back, "Why don't you shut the fuck up." She took a long drag on her cigarette. That did it. I jumped on her remark. "If you don't want to listen or respect the rules, you can walk your butt right out the fucking door." They'd pushed me over the line, but I knew right away I should not have sworn at them.

Lena and I continued arguing and then I lost it with Gabriela, who sat there smirking like some smart-mouth kid. I told her, "Start acting like a responsible teacher." I knew I had to leave the room. I called down to Sylvia and asked her to come up to Gabriela's office. I told the students and Gabriela to stay where they were and not to go to class.

"Sylvia is coming up and we are going to talk about this." Lena responded that she was going to go talk with Sylvia anyway because of how I talked with her.

One of the reasons I wanted Sylvia there is that she smokes in her office, although I've told her it isn't right and sets a bad example for the students. I also hoped she could be a mediator. Lena went off immediately. "It's not fair. We don't get to smoke in the rooms when other people do it. Why is Mark picking on us? It's not fair that when Mark's having a bad day he's allowed to take it out on students. And it's not fair how he talked to Gabriela. She's a teacher and he's treating her like a student."

Sylvia took her on more calmly than I could have at that moment. "It's true there's favoritism about who gets to smoke in their office. I shouldn't smoke in my office either." She pointed out that she doesn't share her office with anyone and that Stuart explicitly asked them to stop. She went into how it creates problems when people make assumptions and then end up "doing their own thing. It reverberates negatively on the students and we give you very mixed messages."

Gabriela took this comment personally and seemed to give the same smirk she gave me. Sylvia called her out. Gabriela said she wasn't smirking, but I don't know if anyone believed her. Lena went back to how I "picked on her and Gabriela." Sylvia said, "Look. Gabriela is not the victim here and she shouldn't become a *cause celebre* of students for supporting you in breaking the rules." Lena asked what the consequences were going to be for my swearing at her. I told her I was wrong and asked what she thought should be done. "You should be suspended just like we would be," she said. "But when have any of you ever been suspended for swearing?" I asked. She countered by saying, "Like you told us at the assembly about teachers who aren't prepared, the consequences should be the same for everyone."

We talked right through second period. By the end, I was drained. Sylvia tried to hammer out an agreement in which we would bring this discussion out into the school. Lena said, "Fine, but it doesn't really matter because nothing is going to change. It'll all just stay the same." I told her this was the third time I'd heard something like that this week. The hopelessness she was expressing really bothered me. She said, "That's the way it is and nothing we can do will change it."

Sylvia asked Lena how she felt during the strike last spring. "Did you believe we could win? If we didn't, we never could have been successful and we wouldn't have this school today." This didn't seem to sway Lena, but we agreed to continue talking in tomorrow's assembly.

I apologized again to the group and to Lena personally for swearing and said I would say the same thing in the assembly.

Sylvia, Gabriela, and I walked down to the second-floor corner office for a surprise birthday lunch for Paul. It was pleasant and low-key until Gabriela jumped on Stuart. "You're an asshole and a snitch for telling Mark about the smoking in our office." He defended himself. "I didn't think I had any other alternative. In fact, I'm glad I did it because now something positive can come from it." Gabriela took her plate of food and walked out of the room.

18

Dancing the Night Away

The moment I walked in the door I was told I had to see Sylvia immediately. Each person I passed asked me if I'd heard what happened. I said no, but no one wanted to be the one to tell me. I sat down in my usual chair next to Sylvia's desk. She said, "There was a party at Gabriela's place last night." She lives in the back part of the school in an agency-subsidized apartment. Sylvia continued. "She invited students and they brought beer and marijuana. Gabriela was also drinking." At around midnight, as the story goes, Gabriela passed out in the bathroom. Because of the loud music, the police came. Students wouldn't let them in so they broke down the door. They told them to keep down the noise and no one was arrested.

Sylvia was livid. She was ready to fire Gabriela on the spot. I suggested we talk to her and hear her version. I agreed that the seriousness of the problem warranted a quick response. We called Gabriela in.

I pulled up an extra chair and Gabriela sat near the door. She admitted to having the party. She did not agree it was inappropriate for a teacher to party and drink with students. "I was on my own time and the students came of their own free will," she told us. "I'd announced in the school last week I was having a house-warming party and no one said anything to me about not inviting students. Where is it written that this is inappropriate behavior for a teacher?" Her argument was that she didn't know and shouldn't be penalized for ignorance.

We spoke to the ethics of being a teacher and why it should be common sense not to drink with underage students. She said that when they came with beer she wasn't going to tell them to go away. "It's your house," Sylvia told her. "At any point you could have said the party was over if they were going to drink alcohol." We questioned her about the police breaking down her door. "Nothing happened and no one was arrested, so what are you worried about?"

Gabriela told us she heard that other teachers in the past had been drinking with students. I said I don't doubt it, but that's not now. Even though it was a difficult discussion, Gabriela raised some points that seemed valid to discuss further, so we proposed a one-week suspension without pay for her to reflect on what happened. She agreed to the suspension, but still didn't think there should be any consequence because she didn't think it was wrong.

I called a staff meeting right after first period to explain the suspension. We met in the second-floor corner office where I explained what I knew about the incident and what happened in our discussion. While we were talking, a set of envelopes appeared under the door. Each of us opened individually addressed protest letters saying the students disagreed with Gabriela's suspension. The letter included a list of six demands. Sylvia could not contain her anger. "What are you going to do?" she asked. As we talked, students started pounding on the door and yelling at us, telling us we shouldn't be meeting by ourselves. We told them we'd be out in a few minutes. We decided to go into the student lounge and meet with the whole school.

All along the hallway were copies of the protest letter taped to the wall.

We, the students of AZTLAN ALTERNATIVE, as young adults, demand an immediate change and clarification upon the alternative high school rules and regulations that have been dictated upon us. The one-week suspension of our peer and friend, Gabriela Rocha, was an undemocratic act of unfairness and an example of the common lack of student input toward decisions affecting the school as a whole. We, the student body, are being exploited and disrespected by being excluded from staff meetings, especially when staff arrogantly decide to be the White Man in our personal lives. This is why we can demand what we want, with full moral authority, what has been stolen from us. This you cannot ignore!

This is a *preliminary* list of our demands:

1. Staff meetings should be open to ALL interested students.

2. Students and staff, as equals, should participate in creating school rules democratically.

3. Educate us, as a school, about other cultures so that we can interact with non-Chicanos without prejudice.

4. Accountability for school funds, in detail.

5. Student participation in the staff hiring process, including volunteer staff.

6. No disciplinary action will be taken against students participating in this protest.

We met with the students. Lisa, Lena, and Tony facilitated the meeting. They confronted us with their demands and challenged us about why we thought we should be able to meet anytime, such as right now, without them. Sylvia explained what had happened with Gabriela and why we made the decision we did. Lena responded quickly. "What students or teachers do on their own time is their own business. Besides, there were other teachers there and you aren't doing anything about them." This was news to me. Robert and Paul, who had not said anything in our staff meeting, admitted they had briefly stopped by the party, but claimed they didn't know about the alcohol or drugs. The students didn't buy this explanation and I didn't blame them.

Tony started jamming Sylvia about how we spend money, like we have some kind of surplus or we're siphoning it off someplace. It wasn't clear to me why they even had this demand. It seemed as though we were going around in circles as Alexis, Stuart, Andrea, and Elena all spoke to why they supported the suspension. We also told them we agreed with their demand about student participation in staff meetings.

I thought we'd be able to go back to class when Lena spoke up again. She said it didn't matter what we did if Gabriela was still suspended. Sylvia explained that this was a personnel matter and non-negotiable. "The entire staff agrees with the decision. Gabriela agreed to accept it, even though she didn't like it. Legally and ethically, what she did was wrong." Lisa responded by saying they have a "right" to party with staff and if we are going to suspend her, we should also suspend them. Sylvia and I said if that's what they want, they can self-suspend themselves. We were ready to go to class.

Sixteen students decided to self-suspend themselves for one day. Like a flashback to last year's strike, the self-suspended students made picket signs and marched in a circle in front of the building. The biggest difference was that now the signs read: "We Have a Right to Party!" Most of the picketers left after other students returned from lunch. We later found out they went up to Gabriela's apartment and some stayed until nearly midnight.

Shortly after I got home, my phone rang. It was Gabriela. She asked me if I was mad at her. I told her no, but I wasn't happy. This is serious and not just because of what she did. I'm also not happy with the students who think it's perfectly fine to drink to excess. I told her we'll talk when she returns next week.

Sylvia and I began our week's end follow-up meeting with Gabriela asking why we needed to talk. Everything was over as far as she was concerned. I told her we wanted to check in, see how she was doing and what she was thinking. "Not much," she said. "I just want to forget about what happened and I think that's what everyone else should do too." Sylvia and I said it wasn't possible to do that because it is still an issue in the school. We need to be able to learn from it.

Sylvia asked Gabriela how she felt about the students going on strike in support of her and why they came up to her apartment after the protest. "They did what they thought was right," she said. "They came up on their own. They came to me as a friend and teacher." Sylvia responded, "Don't you see the power dynamic between them and you? This has to be acknowledged." Gabriela denied there was any kind of empowering. I told her, "You can intellectualize this thing to death and try and deny the power dynamics Sylvia is talking about, but that won't make them disappear." Gabriela shot back, "I still don't know why we're meeting." She was particularly upset that Sylvia was so mad. Sylvia explained that her anger wasn't personal. "But yes, I am angry." She used me as a counterpoint and said I express my feelings more "diplomatically."

I felt that Sylvia and I tried many different ways of reaching out to Gabriela to help her understand what was happening. She remarked, I thought cynically, that we just wanted her to say she was wrong, so she said she was wrong. I told her that didn't cut it because she obviously doesn't believe it. Our discussion ended.

Nothing more was said until Gabriela walked into my office the first day of spring classes. "I'm resigning as of right now," she told me. I was shocked. I wanted to be supportive, but I also knew this was probably best for her and the school. I asked her why. "I'm not happy here anymore." I asked, "What do you want us to tell the students?" "I don't know," she said. I suggested she talk with her advisee group.

The three of us had a final talk in Sylvia's office. Gabriela reached for the box of tissues on Sylvia's desk as she started to cry. "I didn't think this would be so hard," she said. She and Sylvia hugged. She turned to me and we also hugged. I wished her good luck and asked her to stop back at some point. We called an assembly after lunch. Lena announced on behalf of their advisee group that Gabriela was leaving, adding, "But it wasn't because of the students."

19

Student Evaluation Committee

Students only sporadically attended our staff meetings, but they did set up an evaluation committee that sent student representatives to every class. They asked the teacher to leave and then questioned students about the class and the school. They later met with each teacher individually.

We arranged a lunchtime staff meeting at which the committee presented their final report. Their main complaint was that we need to talk with them more about what we are teaching. "Get the curriculum straight in the classes," they told us. They criticized some of the project-based classes. "They aren't teaching us anything. We don't understand what you're trying to do."

They asked for new classes in Criminal Justice, Abnormal Psychology, Home Economics, a men's class, a first-aid class, and a driver's education program. They want every class to have a written syllabus so they know what is expected of them and a list of the reading materials. They said that some teachers tell them they'll give them an "oral syllabus," but that is not acceptable. They feel one reason students get behind in their work is a lack of clarity regarding expectations from the teacher.

The lines of communication between staff and students need improvement. They don't like the fact that we so often do things on short notice. They want us to involve students ahead of time. "Keep pushing us to get involved." They asked for longer advisee groups, "even just 10 more minutes." I asked if they would agree to a longer school day to accommodate this and they thought the students would agree.

Sylvia asked if they had seen any improvements in staff relations. They responded that they feel we're not dwelling on the past as much and we have a more positive attitude. They see a stronger focus on academics and curriculum and think the dynamics among students have improved. There's less tension, more communication, and less personalizing among teachers.

They voiced problems with some of the rules, like beepers and colors. They said some students told them "what we're wearing doesn't affect how we learn." Our staff response was quick. This was non-negotiable because it had to do with physical and emotional safety. The committee also doesn't like the fact that there are consequences for them when they come late, but not for staff. An additional criticism is that we wait until the last minute to face up to problems and confront students when we think they're doing something wrong, like coming back from lunch high.

They asked that teachers talk to students about taking the self-evaluation process more seriously. They think we need to "put our foot down" more. "You play favoritism with some students," they said. They gave the example of Lisa, who has a "license to roam around" while we come down real hard on others.

Lastly, they presented us with a list of other issues that students want addressed. It included the following:

- Need for a student parking lot.
- More student choice in choosing classes.
- Fix up the building.
- Clarification of tuition rules.
- Improving the school's public image.
- More chalk and better chalkboards.
- Too much reliance on traditional teaching methods.
- Need for more student/staff trust.
- Set up a student council.
- Curricular meetings should include student participation.

Their final criticism was that we shouldn't make teachers team-teach if they don't want to. "It works for some classes," Teri said, "but not for others. When it doesn't work, usually one teacher does most of the work or just takes over."

It took a lot of courage for the students to put all of this out to us. Meeting with the whole staff can be intimidating. Robert said later that he felt the students were too negative. Sylvia told him students were expressing "a lot of what they felt. You're being patronizing with your 'we hear this all the time' attitude."

We ended our meeting with the students by agreeing to continue talking with them and to bring the results of the evaluation process into the next assembly for a report and a discussion.

20

Talking with Teachers

I'm tired. But my spirits are up. I like our prospects for next year. I thought it would be good, given that there are only 6 weeks left in the school year, to spend the day talking with the staff.

Elena doesn't have a first-period class. I found her in her office making coffee. She likes her coffee strong. I like strong coffee, but hers is like drinking motor oil. "Our students are our biggest resource," she said. "They give the school its life and purpose." Three months pregnant, she is "confident about next year because this staff is more open to change. I feel we changed things structurally, although we still don't take enough individual initiative. There isn't enough communication taking place to try and understand each others' philosophical and political ideas. It can be exciting to know each others' differences."

Looking at our weaknesses, Elena believes our biggest is "the lack of a background among most of the teachers in alternative education, knowing what it is, and applying it. They fall back on treating this place like a traditional school they attended. They seem to forget we are an alternative program. We always have to try and implement what that means as teachers." Commenting on our small teacher-student ratio, she added, "I don't feel like we're using it to our best advantage right now."

Elena likes the fact that "a majority of students are being challenged by the curriculum this year. The 2-hour class periods are good. Students have the opportunity to become academically engaged. They are utilizing the diversity we have in our staff in a good way. They have identified which staff they can have access to for different things."

Looking ahead, Elena wants us to do more long-term planning. "Philosophical discussions can be so time-consuming. Ideas for our work could better happen in program planning. Good ideas will come out of these kinds of discussions because teachers here are intelligent, energetic people." She would like to "scrap the curricular groups and have schoolwide curricular discussions." Although her baby is due in

November, she plans on teaching as long as she can next fall before taking maternity leave.

I found Paul and Alexis at the photocopy machine copying math assignments. They don't use textbooks, so they have to put together everything they use in class. Looking at the changes we've made this year, Alexis said, "The hardest thing is how much time it takes to come up with new exercises." At the same time, she is "impressed with how well the new students are willing to cooperate and go along with the changes we're trying to implement. It's been the returning students who've complained about working in groups. Some are still complaining about not getting worksheets."

Paul added, "There is still a problem with students not doing homework, although it's better than earlier in the year. They don't think about math after they leave the classroom." Although we abandoned our experiment of making all math classes multilevel, Paul is rethinking how to combine skill levels, "like basic math and pre-algebra or maybe having one class meet at the same time as the next level class."

Looking at the school's strengths, both feel there is more cohesiveness among the staff and in the curriculum. "The overall tone is upbeat and we're better organized," said Alexis. "The previous tension between old and new students is not happening. We have more after-school tutoring and activities, like the ping pong table in the assembly room. Old and new students are hanging around together after school."

The main weaknesses they see are complacency among students and teachers. "We're not living up to our potential yet," said Paul. Both said the key is better communication among staff. "Also, there is still not enough prep time," said Alexis, "especially with the new math changes. We need better time-management skills. We also don't do enough intercurricular planning." Before heading off to class, Paul offered the idea that the student evaluation committee worked well and is a good example of the "need for strong student leadership."

I found Cesar cleaning up the science lab. "I'm doing much better," he said. "I've got the entire session planned out. It's made it easier to evaluate the science activities and given me the chance to focus better, assess the feedback, and get constructive criticism." He thinks the full-staff discussions on curriculum have "made a big difference." At the same time, he is feeling "resentful of some teachers not fulfilling their part." He thinks they see time they are not in class as "free time." He wants staff to do more planning and "generate ideas to get more student involvement in the school." He wonders if "students feel they have a say or if anything will really happen if they propose it."

Cesar stressed that he thinks the greatest strength of the school is the talent of the staff. "Now that we're working better together, the students are giving us a lot less problems. We've got students here who really want to learn and want to be in this kind of educational process. It makes me feel good as a teacher." As far as looking at our weaknesses, he sees "our strong talents not being fully utilized. We ride on our talent. I want us to challenge students more and provide a culture of self-challenge. We need to maintain a high standard of expectations." He would like to see a "common focus" throughout the school, although he's not sure what it should be. "I want us to challenge students culturally, in a community sense, in ways outside of academics, and about their behaviors. We lack a whole-community orientation. I want to see the school be stronger in instilling a sense of community identity and reconnecting students with the community. I want us to re-ask the question: What is the focus of the school?"

I knocked on Patrice's door. "Come in," she called out. The blinds were down and the light off. Talking with her is somewhat problematic these days. She's been in a funk for weeks. Some of it is personal. She has such an attachment to the school, she is like a mother hen to the students. They pick up her moods like a sponge.

Patrice's biggest complaint is that "there is not enough school spirit." She finds staff meetings "feeling less and less serious with too much joking." She sees an overall lack of leadership from staff for the students. "People are too negative." I asked her what she liked about the school right now and she said "our new attendance procedures and our afternoon activities, especially the college prep workshops."

"How do you think we can improve school spirit, Patrice?" "I would start with awards," she said, "including teachers. And competitions, a spelling contest, inviting other schools over to visit, volleyball on the boulevard at lunch and after school, and swimming at the park." Animation reappeared in her voice. "Go for it," I tell her. "I will," she said. I opened her blinds to let in some light as I left. She didn't object.

After getting a coconut *paleta* from the vendor in front of school, I head up to the corner office to see Manuel and Andrea. We immediately get into talking about curriculum. Manuel said, "I'm trying group projects in World History, but I don't think they're working too well." I had earlier suggested an atlas project for a geography lesson he wanted to do. "I let them choose their own groups, but I didn't know what to do when the groups weren't working."

In his Mexican History I class, Manuel "started with relevant student themes" such as stereotypes, family structure, and identity. "I have tried to make it personal and a shared link into a study of the

Olmecas. In U.S. History, I am focusing on family structures and the police. My theme is justice. I'm beginning with the students' experiences with the police. I ask them: What is myth and what is reality?" One dramatic change in all his social studies classes is that he has abandoned a "chronological approach to teaching history."

For the whole school, Manuel says, "One of our main strengths is the serious tone we are now setting for the students. Individual teachers are more into their classes and classes are more serious. There is better preparation and students have responded positively. We've had too much of a relaxed atmosphere, which led to laziness from both staff and students."

Looking at our weaknesses, Manuel named the "inequities" in how we've dealt with students. "We have to be consistent." He sees "less friction" among staff and believes we should "junk" the earlier part of the year. His main priority is to have another round of discussion about a Mexican-centric curriculum and he's thinking about writing a paper for everyone to read.

Andrea said her decision not to come back next year has "helped me be a better teacher." She thought about a comment I made to her in a curricular meeting earlier this year that she is more of a teacher-centered teacher than a student-centered teacher. She now thinks this is true. "I'm trying to change. In the Spanish classes I'm bringing in different reading materials. I'm using puzzle books and having more conversations and dialogues, especially with the advanced students." She's attempting to do more with projects that incorporate reading, writing, and conversation rather than comprehension exercises. One of her projects is making puppets and using them to "create scenarios." She finds it easier to work with newer students because "old students are too used to what I did before and don't want to try new things."

Andrea thinks that "communication is now one of our strengths. We are more consistent and trying to work better together. We sit down and talk more. We're not getting caught up in the little stuff so much." Balancing this with our weaknesses, she sees "a lack of time-management skills across the board, our inability to have parent meetings, and too much paperwork." For priorities, Andrea suggests that we "concentrate more on getting resources for the school," such as a higher-quality copy machine and better computers.

Classes had just ended when there was a knock at my office door. Robert stuck his head in. "I hear you're talking with all the teachers." Robert tends to take things personally and may be feeling left out. "Yeah," I said, "come on in and have a seat."

Robert began by saying he thinks that "communication among

staff is better." He is encouraged that the "less-experienced staff are now playing a bigger role." He sees the strengths of the school as "students getting to make their own choices and how we don't demand that students all do the same things. It is important how we have personal relationships with each of the students and that we expose them to Chicano literature."

Robert sees our main weakness as "lack of communication." He is not a fan of the "project-oriented approach" and doesn't believe it is working well. "The students don't see the immediacy." He favors the kinds of "final projects I use in English."

Looking at priorities, Robert cites "communication among advisors" as his main one. This being Robert, he focused on what he considers to be a strong point of his, advisee work, and used it as a springboard for both complaining and putting himself forward as an example. "We should help students have more of a voice in the school." He also wants us to focus on developing more intercurricular programs.

My final discussion of the day was with Stuart. We sat on the large library windowsills facing out onto the boulevard. "Things are getting better," he said. "I've noticed I'm being stricter in my classes. I'm not so worried anymore about whether students like me or not. My main focus is teaching, having a good learning experience in the classroom, and being better prepared. I am setting higher expectations for students, almost to the freshman level of college." He thinks that for some of our students "the curriculum is too watered down. I want to figure out better ways to individualize curriculum."

Looking at staff relations, Stuart is upbeat. "We're starting to cooperate better as a staff. People are trying to be more serious and getting students to focus more." He commented that staff are starting to be "real" teachers. "Earlier in the year, the new teachers were working real hard to be liked and that created problems." Stuart's priority for next year is "developing some form of community service for students. I want more of a focus on getting students outside of the school so they can see other options. We need to make our expectations high, stressing academics, responsibility, and positive behavior."

As for our weaknesses, Stuart is most unhappy with the "team-teaching thing," which isn't working out for him. He sees teachers looking back too much at "how they learned things. We need to be learning more about teaching. I believe if we worked harder as a staff, it would lead to everything flowing better and better communication. We need to work to trust each other more." Stuart looked at his watch and realized he had to leave to get to his night job on time.

21

The Retreat

The past 9 months have felt like a birthing process. Painful, traumatic, hopeful, exhilarating at times, with tears, laughter, heartache, lots of sweat and hard work. But we finally made it. It now looks as though we will have the same staff next year minus Gabriela and Andrea, plus we'll have Alberto, who is returning from his sabbatical. We're no longer fighting with each other. We've built a trust that can come only through common experience. Our staff unity has not totally manifested itself with the students, but, like an early sunrise, light has begun to appear.

Students asked for an all-school trip. We proposed a 3-day, 2-night retreat at a cooperative camp deep in the forest about 5 hours outside the city. We'd been planning it for nearly a month. Everyone was excited and some of the young mothers brought their children. A staff-student committee planned fun and serious activities and the weather looked sensational for late spring. As it turned out, our birthing process was not yet complete. At its best and its worst, the retreat took all of our collective strength and served to rally a majority of students to fight for the integrity of the school.

THE BOULEVARD WAS covered with a light dew that was quickly burning off in the morning sun. Most of the teachers arrived by 7:30. Late yesterday we rented four 15-passenger vans, two bright red, one blue, and one white. We lined them up on the street in preparation for our exit from the city. About 20 students were here early with us, but as seems to be our tradition, we did not get started on time. Last-minute permission slips, setting up seating arrangements, figuring out our travel route—we dragged on until 9:00 before nearly 70 people piled into the vans and Paul's truck.

Caravanning up the highway with Elena's van in the lead and Paul's truck bringing up the rear, we talked, listened to music, and sang songs in English and Spanish. With eight kids under the age of 3, we seemed to stop at every rest area. Finally, in mid-afternoon, we found our exit and headed into the forest. Past cattle farms and rolling hills, we traversed the countryside. The last gravel-and-dirt road took us to the camp.

It was a beautiful day. The temperature rose to the high 60s, the sky was clear, and the students and their children looked beautiful and happy. This was the best I'd felt in months. The camp directors greeted us and we held a short orientation session before setting up in the small cabins and dormitory.

The students were divided by gender. The male staff met with the male students. Two-thirds of the men and three teachers will share the second floor of the dorm. The rest of the male students, Cesar, and I hiked off to the unheated four-person cabins. The women set up on the first floor of the dorm and two of the cabins adjacent to ours. The mothers and children were given priority in the dorm.

We set up a work chart according to advisee groups. Elena's group prepared a late lunch while the rest of us explored the camp. The first inkling of trouble surfaced when we heard a rumor that some of the male students were getting high in their dorm room.

After our lunch snack we called everyone together for another meeting. Students ran down the schedule and we reiterated the camp rules. I got up and made a special announcement about the rumor we'd heard, which students denied. I continued by explaining that everyone agreed back at school that there would be no drugs or alcohol on this trip. "This will serve as the one and only warning," I said. From there, we announced a hike to the lake.

Ten minutes later, we gathered and took off. It's about half a mile to the sandy beach on the small lake next to a national forest. There were about 25 of us and 4 young children. Almost everyone got into the water, which wasn't all that warm even though the air felt comfortable. The students were like young kids, frolicking, playing tag in the water, splashing each other. It was a fun beginning. Robert, as only Robert can do, showed up in a bikini bathing suit to the embarrassment of almost everyone. It showed off his paunch and made him an easy target for student ridicule, but he took it in stride and helped create a festive atmosphere. I had to leave with students from my advisee group 45 minutes later because my group and Alexis's had dinner setup. The hike back was all uphill and, city folks that we were, we were exhausted when we got back to the farmhouse where the kitchen is located and meals are eaten communally.

The common meal room held 16 wooden picnic tables and benches. We took the benches off the tops of the tables and cleaned the table tops. We put out the silverware, napkins, water pitchers, and serving utensils. Martha rang the farmhouse bell. The room began to fill, although I noticed that Manuel, Cesar, and Alexis were missing. We waited about 5 minutes. I called the room to order. I explained the rituals and routines of the camp, including how one person at each table serves, and everyone clears their tables for the clean-up crew. There was some grumbling from students who were designated servers, but they agreed to go along with the camp policies.

As the kitchen doors opened, we waited in anticipation for the promised homemade lasagna with garlic bread and salad. What we found in the server bowls were hamburgers and hot dogs with chips and watermelon. The burgers were small and tasteless. The buns were whole wheat and not a hit with students. Although this turned out to be a miscommunication with the kitchen staff, we were a hungry group. It created a restlessness that was aggravated when Cesar, Manuel, and Alexis arrived about 15 minutes into dinner. Manuel and Cesar sat at my table and started joking with students, leaning over other tables to get food, and carrying on like they were teenagers. I almost anticipated a food fight erupting.

When it was time to clean up, I had to yell to get everyone's attention. It didn't work. Manuel saw my frustration, turned to me, laughed, and said, "Don't worry, they're just animals. Give it a break." I was taken aback, but decided to try to relax. The students seemed happy. The joking continued as students filed out and the clean-up groups began clearing tables and washing dishes.

Half an hour later we broke up into small groups based on advisee groups. We agreed to discuss and develop proposals on the question: If you were going to set up a school, what would it look like, what would be taught, how would it be governed? Elena's group joined mine because Teri's baby had a high fever so they took her to the nearest hospital. She returned just in time for the campfire.

Earlier in the evening, Robert and his advisee group gathered paper and wood. We were met at a circular clearing near the apple orchard with a blazing fire. Manuel became our master of ceremonies and regaled us with ghost stories and psychic events. It was a real show. There was no one else in the camp so we gave students the freedom to wander and do as they pleased.

After the campfire I hung out with the teachers near the farmhouse where small groups of students joined us from time to time. We played a game of cooperative kick the can. I eventually headed off to the cabins with Patrice. We met some of the women students, who wanted to move up into the dorms where it was warmer. We walked back up with them and three students agreed to switch to the cabins. I met Cesar on one of the hiking paths as we both headed to our cabin around 1:00 A.M. We stopped to talk with some of the young men who were playing cards under a flashlight hung from a tree branch. We finally bedded down around 2:30.

I woke up a little before 7:00. It was a beautiful morning. The sun glistened through the trees as I hiked up to the farmhouse. I walked in, said hello to the kitchen staff, got myself a cup of coffee, and sat on the wooden deck. What a life. Too bad we can't have a school that's as safe and tranquil as being up here. Looking off to the forest, I noticed Elena heading toward me from the dorms. As I greeted her, she said, "We've got a big problem." "What's wrong?" I asked. As the sordid tale unfolded, I felt the peacefulness sink out of my body.

Students partied long into the night, listening to music, dancing, and talking. All seemed to be fine until the staff were asleep. Then, about 20 students took off for the woods. What we later found out is they conspired to make us think there had been no drugs or alcohol. In actuality, they were drinking and smoking marijuana, and some dropped acid. One of the dorm rooms was set aside for students who wanted to have sex. About 3:00 A.M., the woods group decided it would be fun to purposely get lost in the forest. Running through the trees, they came across a house where the owner came out and chased after them with a shotgun.

The teachers in the dorm thought that students had violated all of the agreed-upon rules. There was no reason to stay. The offenders should immediately be dropped from school. When the students who weren't involved heard we might all leave, they protested and said it wasn't fair to the ones who weren't getting high or running around.

The staff met and we agreed to call an all-school meeting after breakfast. We would try to have a discussion with the students and if the ones who were high would cop to it, we would load up a van and drive them back to the school. The other students could stay and finish out the retreat. We required everyone to be present at breakfast. The mood was quiet and sullen. The food was better. We had pancakes with pure maple syrup from camp trees. After breakfast clean-up, Patrice rang the bell and we gathered back in the meal room.

Elena facilitated the discussion. She laid out what had happened and asked for input from students. They were slow to respond. Natalia and Eloisa said it wasn't fair to send everyone back when only some students broke the rules. Johnny stood up and criticized those who got high. "Why couldn't you leave it alone for one night?" This got a nasty response from his fellow gang members and could lead to some kind of violation, but it took courage to speak out. Rosa said she didn't like the fact that people were getting high when "we had our children and babies here." Lena was upset that one of the people high was a mother who had someone else watching her child. "You should be taking care of your own babies." This brought a quick retort from another mother who wasn't high, but said "the mothers are not the ones you should be mad at."

None of the students seemed willing to offer ideas on consequences, so I made a proposal. "Those students who didn't get high, how about if you get up and walk out to the wooden deck. Those who did, you stay here. If you leave, but your adviser thinks you are one of the people who got high, you will be asked to come back to the dining room. We need to be honest about what happened last night and create our own process for resolving it. Those who did get high will have to leave camp. You will also be suspended until September. You do have the right to petition to return to school sooner." I stated that the consequence for those who don't come forward would be more severe, although I wasn't specific. I ended by saying, "If this does not work, we are prepared to load up the vans and all return home."

We were met with silence. Students looked at each other. Finally, Teri stood up and said, "Look, you know who you are. I'm not afraid to say your names if that's what you want." Roberto got up from his bench. "Fuck it. Just leave. I was out there last night. I admit it." Most students got up and walked out of the room, leaving nine bodies sitting at the tables. As Patrice and I began to talk with them, three more students walked back in from outside.

Although none of the teachers wanted to leave, Patrice and I volunteered. She told the students to pack up their belongings and check in with their advisers. "We'll meet you at the van in 20 minutes." We knew there were more students involved last night, but we had a full van.

We left around 10:00 A.M. and the students were not friendly to us on the ride back. We were nice enough to them, I thought. We stopped three times, played their tapes, and didn't get on them at all. Plus, we were tired and it was a long haul. They sang Cypress Hill songs and goaded us about their right to get high and party. When we got back, they left in a group and didn't come into the school.

The following Monday afternoon, the staff met to discuss the fate of the 12 and what to do with others who hadn't come forward. Patrice and I were particularly unhappy with the group we drove back because they have been saying we "mistreated" them because we weren't "friendly" during the ride. To us, they seemed to be taking little responsibility for their actions.

Andrea walked in late to our meeting and said she had been talking with Roberto, who now claims he wasn't high at the retreat. This brought a chorus of groans. He has been identified as the person who brought most of the drugs and we have been told he was "flying higher than a kite." Andrea jumped on us for being disrespectful and judgmental. Manuel tried to explain to her why we were responding this way, but she didn't want to hear it. Sylvia proposed that all 12 stay out of school until September, but they be automatically allowed back in. I objected to the automatic coming back part without some kind of process, but we couldn't agree on what the process would be.

We were perplexed about what to do about students we thought participated, but who have not come forward. Among us we had five additional names. We decided to announce during tomorrow's advisee groups and Wednesday's assembly that we are giving students a 48-hour window of opportunity to come forward. For the next 2 days, they will receive the same consequences as the ones who came forward at the retreat. If they don't and we believe they participated, the consequences will be more severe.

I'm not happy with this process, but I don't see any viable alternatives. Two students came forward, both at the end of the second day. Rightly or wrongly, we didn't finger anyone else. Their consciences will have to be their guides.

Following the retreat, the last 3 weeks of school felt like a boulder had been lifted off our shoulders. We had no problems and ended the year with a beautiful graduation ceremony at the local fieldhouse.

Guidepost

After a full year of work together and a summer away to personally reflect on our roles in the school, our unity was high. We were a more mature and experienced staff as we embarked on our last 10 months together. We saw a bright future ahead as we envisioned this process extending over the next few years. We set out to make the students our primary concern and focus and collaborated more in our teaching and preparation through small curricular groups. Alberto returned from his sabbatical and his presence signified a coming together of politics, spirituality, and cross-generational cooperation that shaped our early meetings.

During the summer, the board of directors of the agency hired a new executive director, Adolfo Amaro. Elena was our designated member of the search committee and it looked as though they had chosen someone we could work with and who would support the direction of the school.

Unfortunately, fate dealt us a bad hand. Adolfo brought with him a partner, Alfredo Rivera, and a hierarchical philosophy of management and a personal mandate to shift the focus of the high school to a traditional GED program and away from any form of democratic or student participation. Personally, I became a buffer between the high school and the administration when I was "ordered" to join the management team. Representing the high school and being white led to a series of confrontations between Adolfo and me that shaped much of the battle for the whole school as we sought to preserve what we had built. Our abilities to teach, serve students, and fight to save the school stretched our resources and energies to the breaking point. The final Aztlan Alternative stories relate our attempts to make peace among ourselves, organize to keep the school alive, and transition into what the inevitable handwriting on the wall told us would be our last days together.

22

Another Beginning

Summer has dragged into September with a vengeance. It is so hot in my office that sweat drips onto my keyboard as I type on the computer. A T-shirt, shorts, and sandals are about all anyone can wear. We held a new-student orientation in the assembly room in the early evening and it felt like a group sauna. At about 9:00 I head out to the parking lot. The temperature is still in the high 80s. The humidity is so severe it's hard to breathe. Families trying to survive the heat outnumber the gang members on the boulevard, making it look like a refugee camp. I cross the street into the gravel parking lot, past the unenforced warning that it is only for Aztlan Alternative employees. The only available parking space this morning was next to the alley near a line of six garbage cans. I don't usually park here because of the rats, but I haven't seen many lately. Big mistake.

As I approach my car, I hear scurrying. I stop, look down, and rats run right in front of me. I jump back. Other nights I've worked late I've had rats run over my feet as I opened my car door, but I've always had on boots or hard shoes. There was no way I was going up against these rats in sandals. I call them monster rats. They're bigger than any cat. Stuart had an encounter one morning with one perched on the microwave. He yelled at it, stomped on the floor, banged on the door. It still wouldn't leave.

I try four times to approach my car, but I can't get close enough to unlock the door. I bang on the trunk, kick up the gravel. I even try talking to them. People in the neighborhood must have thought this was one crazy white guy. On my last try, I turn the key, hop in, and slam the door behind me. Victory. Maybe. They still own the parking lot. I'm just a visitor.

THE HIGH SCHOOL STAFF is off to a great start. Alberto has returned from his sabbatical looking less haggard and more full of life. Elena is 7 months pregnant. She wants to work with the teachers and her advisees, but not be assigned any classes. Cesar, Alexis, Manuel, Robert, and Stuart are back and we hired Angel Muñoz as a new Spanish and video arts teacher. Patrice is still our registrar. The board of directors hired a new executive director, Adolfo Amaro, so Sylvia's duties are being redefined and she's talking about possibly teaching a couple of Chicano Studies classes. I've proposed that I teach full-time again. It may be a mistake, but I want to be in the classroom more and we need the teachers, although I'm worried other parts of the program will suffer. I have told the staff this will work only if everyone takes up some of my day-to-day responsibilities, such as attendance and monitoring the halls. Everyone agreed.

The mood of the staff is positive, especially given the intense heat. We've matured over the summer. We're all talking to each other and there's a healthy pragmatism in our approach. Even in the always agonizing discussion of which applicants to accept and which to turn away because we don't have space, we respected each other's opinions and managed to come up with compromises that everyone can live with.

Throughout the first 2 weeks we held curricular discussions in small groups and as a whole staff. At Elena's suggestion, we tried to focus on reaching common understandings on content, methodology, and available and needed resources. We talked about different kinds of teaching methods that we use here including lecture, small group, individual work, projects, and large-group discussions. I emphasized that whatever methods we use, we want to complement one another.

Cesar asked for opinions on how we identify and respond to individual student needs and interests. Manuel and Robert both responded that we can't answer this question until we ask students. I felt uncomfortable with this because it seemed like a cover for "I don't have to prepare because I can't really do anything until I know what the students want to learn." Alberto asked that we focus on reading because we know students are going to come in with vast differences in their abilities and it affects every subject area.

We agreed immediately that assessment is a problem. We are required by our funders to give both pre and post standardized reading tests that are normed to incarcerated adult learners. We're not happy with giving the tests and use them only as a reference in assessing skills. Last year, I started teaching a voluntary class for students with low reading levels. I previously tried assigning lower-skilled readers to the class, but they said it made them feel they were back in public school in the "dummy classes." Just making it voluntary seemed to solve the problem. We also quickly discovered the need to teach reading in Spanish to the native Spanish speakers as a vehicle toward achieving literacy in both Spanish and English.

It may seem self-evident, but our other discovery was that students who did not like to read or who had low reading skills blossomed when given interesting material. Elena and I began developing our own canon of culturally relevant and age-appropriate books for Aztlan Alternative students. It was always a thrill to watch young people in their late teens finish their first novels.

In our discussion of homework we wanted to avoid the trap we fell into last year with some teachers allowing students to get away with doing none. It didn't help the students and it set a bad precedent for other teachers. We sought to redefine the purpose of homework. We wanted to make it important for its own sake and not busywork. It must be purposeful. Everyone agreed to incorporate homework into their classes in some way. We're thinking of experimenting with having homework buddies and homework books to keep track of student work and assignments.

One of the biggest surprises for me came during a discussion of writing across the curriculum. Manuel said some students had complained to him that we don't teach enough grammar and sentence structure. He characterized our writing approach as "liberal." When pushed, he admitted he was taught to write by "focusing on the basics." It became a chicken-and-egg argument. As Manuel explained, "Some students need it because they say they can't write without these skills." Although we've proven the opposite in the writing classes, we did agree that our approach may not work with everyone. In the end, Manuel seemed to change his opinion, reluctantly admitting that students are writing more and the quality of their work is improving.

Our first potential crisis came when it was discovered in the middle of scheduling that we needed to switch around some of the classes. Contrary to how we would have approached this last year, we persevered and got it done without much tension. We joked and compromised when we hit a logjam. We're starting out the year with 88 students.

MAYBE CRISES ARE endemic to this place; it didn't take long for the first major one to appear. Sylvia called me into her office. Sitting back in her chair, the door closed and the window open while she smoked, she updated me on the problems she's been having with Adolfo. He has demanded that she change her management style and set up a corporate-type evaluation process for the high school. He won't let her teach and is insisting she not discuss their management team meet-

ings with me or anyone else. During the past year, Sylvia has acted as
the de facto interim executive director and set up what she calls a flat
management structure. Adolfo has made it clear that he is the "leader"
of the agency and wants no dissension. Sylvia is an outspoken person
and the two have clashed since their first meetings.

"I've been talking with my husband and my friends," Sylvia said,
"about what I've had to put up with since July. They're asking me why
I stay here and put up with this abuse. I've finally reached the point
where I don't want to deal with it anymore. I'm tired and emotionally
drained." Sylvia has told me before that she felt like quitting, but she
has an internal resiliency that has always kept her coming back. "I'm
ready to leave," she said. "I'm going to turn in my resignation, effective
September 16, Mexican Independence Day. My last day will be Friday."

I respect Sylvia for her decision. She's done a lot for this place. She
held it together after the strike and is well liked throughout the agency,
except by the business office. Sylvia believes part of the problem is the
men who head the business office and the agency who have a hard
time dealing with a Chicana who sticks up for herself. I would agree. I
also think she has a more progressive philosophy and is willing to listen to others, which you can't say about a lot of the men around here.
This is going to be a great personal loss to me and I worry what its
impact will be on the high school program.

Sylvia asked for a staff meeting at lunch. We sat in shocked silence.
Because we're off to a good start, I get the feeling we don't yet understand the significance of her leaving. I'm already feeling overwhelmed,
especially with Elena being out for the next couple of months.

On Friday we held an agency going-away party for Sylvia. All of
the "line staff," as we are now called, attended. The only one from
management to show up was Daniel Matos, a recent college graduate
and the youngest manager. He told me he has been designated to over-
see the high school. Alberto brought out the sage and conducted a
going-away ceremony before blessing the food laid out on two tables in
the middle of the assembly room. The women from child care had offered to do the cooking and they produced quite a spread. The cake
was huge and written in icing were the words, *Adios y Buena Suerte*
(Goodbye and Good Luck). Sylvia packed up the last of her office and
was out of the building by 3:00.

At 3:15, the rest of us, or at least those who showed up, were at our
first all-staff meeting with Adolfo. His initial words were "We bought a
cake and flowers for Sylvia, but we can't find her." Dressed in an expen-
sive suit and tie, unusual dress for around here, he said, "I sent out a
memo stating these meetings are mandatory. Starting today, anyone

who does not have a legitimate excuse will be docked pay for not attending." He informed us that he had hired a consultant, Alfredo Rivera, to work with him to "change the direction of Aztlan Alternative. I know there are certain people who don't want to agree with my program. You should start looking for new employment." The tone was harsh. I took it as a threat. Staff know he is capable of firing people because he has already fired two staff members from social services. The "talk" in the agency is that Sylvia was forced out and did not leave of her own accord.

I must admit, I wasn't clear on what was happening as I watched Adolfo pace the student lounge. His body language and words give the clear impression that you are either with him or against him. I sat in amazement as Julia, from social services, stood up and said, "It's great that now we can communicate with each other honestly." I had the opposite feeling, but I kept my mouth shut. Dissent, or even discussion, seemed out of the question and was effectively quelled just by the tone.

After the meeting, I went in to talk with Daniel. I asked him what was happening and what he thinks all this will mean for the high school. "When Sylvia was here, I was laid back and didn't say much," he told me, "but now I feel comfortable speaking up." He defended Adolfo's tone. "He doesn't talk like that in the management team meetings. He was just nervous. I told Adolfo he should write down what he's going to say before he says it." Why does this feel like damage control? I'm not sure where Daniel is coming from or whether I can trust him. He was hired by Oscar shortly before the strike and tried to play both sides, which hasn't endeared him to the high school staff.

A FEW DAYS after classes started, we sat together in the library at our weekly staff meeting. Stuart offhandedly asked, "What's up with the federal cabinet official coming to visit?" Cesar asked, "Who?" No one knew what he was talking about. Stuart told us that the social services manager came up to him this morning, asking him to set up a class to showcase the high school for the "Clinton guy." "He's coming next Wednesday. I was told the U.S. Marshals will be here checking out the place and doing security checks on everyone who works here."

This threw the high school staff into a frenzy. We didn't like the secrecy or the circumvention of the high school's policies about visitors. And we were not happy about this person coming here in the first place. Who was he, what was his purpose, and what's with the security checks of staff? Daniel happened to walk into our meeting at that moment and got an earful. He said he knew about the visit and was going to tell us, but hadn't had time. He offered to talk with Adolfo. "I'll find out more information and then come to your assembly in the morning."

The next day, I ran into Daniel as I entered the building. He told me he agreed that the process around the visit wasn't good, although he doesn't agree with our negative feelings about the purpose of the visit. He said he and Adolfo would come to the assembly.

When I walked into the assembly room, Daniel and Adolfo were already seated. I talked to Cesar, who was facilitating, and suggested we begin with Adolfo since this is the first time he has attended an assembly or met with the students. I told Adolfo, whom I had yet to talk with other than a formal introduction, that I would introduce him, but it would be good if he could say something about himself and open it up for questions before we get into the discussion of the upcoming visit.

Adolfo stood in front of the students, again dressed in a high-quality suit, and said, "I am a homeboy just like you. I'm from the barrio in Texas. See these tattoos?" He raised his sleeves and pointed to his arms. This brought yells from some of the male students, who called out their gang names, something we would normally never tolerate, but we let it slide. "I am a revolutionary," he said. Speaking to the "brothers" in the room, he walked over to the group of students who yelled. "I know what it's about," he said, doing hands-on-the-hips, gang-type posturing. I found all this somewhat embarrassing to listen to, but I figure he's going to have to make his own way with the students.

Adolfo turned to me and asked that I say why the "teachers don't want" the federal official coming to the high school. I gave an overview of our policies regarding visitors. "We ask that they be participants and not just observers. This is a policy initiated by students, who have made it clear in the past they don't want to feel like they are in a zoo." My next words got me in more trouble than I bargained for. "We don't allow people to come in here and pimp off of the students."

Adolfo, standing to my side, moved in front of me, clearly sending a message that he is in charge and it was his turn to speak. "The reason I am here today is I have been fronted off by the high school teachers who didn't come to me first. I am a revolutionary and I don't pimp off nobody." He pulled out his wallet and said, "It's all about what I've got in here. See this suit? Who do you think pays for what I've got? Who do you think pays the teachers? We live in a capitalist society. You have to realize we wouldn't have any money or good clothes without using the system." Walking again over to the grouping of male students, he pointed back toward the teachers and said, "There will be no self-serving motherfuckers in this agency. They think they are revolutionaries. Until they go to the mountains, like I have, they don't know shit about revolution. If there are any protests or disruptions during this visit, there won't be a high school anymore."

I was aghast. I can't believe what he called us—in front of the students no less. I didn't say another word. A small group of women students challenged him. "Why don't you go along with the high school's traditions of talking about visitors before they come into the school?" Adolfo responded, "Those are old traditions. Now, I make the rules. There are going to be new traditions." When asked about the federal marshals being in the school and how this was against out school policy of no police in the building, he repeated his proclamation that he is now making the rules.

The teachers were left dazed. It was lunchtime, but we all headed to the library to talk. Manuel was sharpest in his criticism, saying we should boycott the visit. Cesar asked what it says to the community to have police in the school. Stuart said we didn't have any choice. "We should just go along like it's a regular school day and treat it as no big deal." We all agree that Adolfo is serious about coming down hard on the high school. We don't like it, but we don't have the enthusiasm for another big confrontation with the administration at this point in time. Leaving work that day, I saw Daniel, who told me we should "go along with the program. If you don't, people will lose their jobs."

The following morning, students called an emergency meeting to talk about yesterday's assembly. They are "ready to go out on strike" to get rid of Adolfo. They asked why Sylvia can't come back and take his place. Other students argued that there wasn't much we could do about the upcoming visit, that it is a done deal. Jason is particularly angry about the federal marshals. He said he heard they are going to check all the student lockers.

Manuel and I spoke for the staff. We urged calm and presented the idea of doing a business-as-usual thing next Wednesday and not doing anything special about the visit. I don't know if we were very convincing, but students agreed to go along.

THE DAY BEFORE the visit, the board president came to see me. I'd been laying low, teaching class and staying upstairs in my office. She was cordial and I avoided anything controversial, waiting for her to initiate the discussion. She didn't mention what Adolfo said about the teachers at the assembly and I'm assuming she doesn't know. She asked me about federal funding opportunities for the high school. I told her, honestly, that I do not know what kinds of monies are available. She finally raised the issue of tomorrow's visit and the need for the agency to pursue a long-term strategy for getting federal monies. She emphasized to me the need for tomorrow to go well and for there not to be any protests or demonstrations. I assured her the high school was not going to disrupt the proceedings.

The morning of the visit we held an assembly. Elena led the discussion, asking everyone how they felt. Most of the talk was negative. As we broke up to return to classes, we saw the first marshals, four tall white men in dark suits standing in front of the building, looking very out of place, talking into small microphones in their hands and looking nervous. An array of politicians began filing into the assembly room.

The only confrontation came when a busload of students from the nearby high school, the one many of our students previously attended, arrived and were escorted into the building. They had been "invited" by the youth leadership program operated by social services. A half-dozen Aztlan Alternative students who worked with the project were also allowed into the room. Our students said the other students had all of the seats. They were told to sit on the floor, off to the side. They thought that what the other students said were lies and didn't honestly reflect what was happening in the community. None of our students were called on to speak.

I stayed upstairs in my office. Out of sight, out of mind. After the visit, as I was leaving the building, Daniel found me and said, "Some of your students were abusive to the other high school students. Management and the board are upset. Adolfo is issuing written reprimands to all the high school staff." I was mad. "What kind of process is this? Don't you even want to know how our students felt?" I knew some students had verbally harassed some of the other students, but I didn't feel like giving in. He finally agreed to ask Adolfo to come to a staff meeting. He then told me that Adolfo ordered metal clamps attached to all the windows. They will no longer open more than 6 inches because students were seen leaning out of them during the visit. By the next morning, all the windows facing the street had been clamped. By mid-afternoon, students unscrewed more than half the clamps.

When Adolfo came to our staff meeting, he said "I am disappointed in the behavior of the high school students." He told us he went to apologize to an assembly at the public high school. "I was embarrassed to say I was from Aztlan Alternative. But since I am the top person here I knew I had to go. You teachers don't provide any discipline. You're not giving the students an education. They are easily manipulated. You are the instigators, so I blame you." The only positive note was that he said he would keep the reprimands on hold. It felt as though we were being put on probation, although this was not said.

As Adolfo got up to leave, he said to me, "We have set in motion the MRT, the Management Response Team. We met and the chain of command is in place. Daniel is now in charge of the high school." Turning to the teachers, he said, "You will report to Mark. Mark will report to Daniel. Daniel will report to me." Management Response Team? Might as well change that to Military Response Team because it feels like a military coup.

23

Face to Face with Adolfo

Things seem to have calmed down somewhat the past week. It's about 3:30 and I'm walking down the stairs to wash out my coffee pot. I pass Alfredo. I knew him years ago when he was a political activist. At the time, we were on friendly terms. Alfredo generally looks sharp in his dark suits and sparkling white shirts. Today he looks beleaguered. His hair is ruffled, his neck is sweaty, and his oversized belly is hanging over his belt. He asks how I'm doing. I say, "I've been better, but I'm okay. It's a long story." He said, "I heard you're in the middle of a lot of things around here." "Not that I know of," I respond. "I'm just trying to do my best." As he turned to walk down the stairs, he looked at me sternly. "You have to choose where you stand, Mark. Are you going to be a leader or are you going to stand in the way." I started to say "Between you and me, Alfredo. . . ." He cut me off. His face reddened as he angrily shouted, "I am not a go-between who passes messages." Adolfo and Daniel walked through the door. I was in the middle of telling Alfredo I didn't expect him to be a go-between. "All I said was between you and me." Adolfo looked at me. "I want to see you in my office at 1:30," he said. He took me by surprise. I looked at my watch. "Today? It's already past 1:30." He sarcastically replied, "No, at 1:30 in the morning." I told Adolfo I am here and can meet any time. He said he and Daniel will meet with me now.

I followed the two of them into Adolfo's office. We sat in three chairs in front of the power desk, with me in the middle. Adolfo began the conversation. "I am giving you a verbal warning. You will receive a written reprimand tomorrow in your personnel file." I didn't know how to respond, so I said "Why?" Adolfo continued. "You've been going around back-stabbing me, calling me a dictator, and saying that I'm as bad as Oscar was as executive director." I asked where he got this information. He wouldn't say, but he told me he heard this about both Elena and myself.

I was trying to do my best yoga breathing while I attempted to figure out what was going on. Adolfo went on to say, "Your high school is for shit. You are sabotaging what I'm doing. If you don't stop, I'll fire you or you can quit. That assembly you made me come to was a set-up. That was chicken shit. You set me up. Those students only mouth what they are told by the teachers. They don't think for themselves. It was your agenda they're pushing. I won't stand for this."

Daniel sat there, not saying a word. Adolfo leaned toward me, pointing his finger at my face. "I'll tell you in private what I really think of you." I told him, "I have nothing to hide. Go ahead and say it in front of Daniel." "Okay," he said. "You're a liberal, rich, white motherfucker. You're a pimp. You just take from the community and give nothing back." I told him he could make whatever assumptions he wanted but he didn't know me.

I was getting angry. But he'd caught me off guard and I wanted to hear him out. Adolfo said there was going to be no more gossip in this agency. I told him, "The accusations you are making against me are bullshit. You can believe what you want, but you have to recognize you are also challenging my integrity. If you hear that I've said something, come to me first. If it's true, Adolfo, I'll give you my resignation on the spot."

Adolfo responded, "From now on, you will be held personally responsible for anything that goes wrong in the high school." I tried to explain to him that the essence of my position was one of a principal within a cooperative staff. "I like it that way and don't want to be part of a chain of command." He looked down at the papers in his lap, then back up at me. "You called me a dictator. Now, you're going to get a dictator. This organization needs discipline and I'm the one to give it."

Daniel said he wanted to speak. "Adolfo is speaking for himself, but I agree with what he is trying to do for the agency." He said he also doesn't believe the high school students think for themselves. "They just mouth other peoples' agendas and are easily influenced." I tried to explain to both of them that we are trying to help students unlearn some of the ways they are taught to think in public school. "Our work is based in helping them acquire tools of critical thinking. Part of the process of using those tools is unlearning some of the things they learned before. Here they get to take this new knowledge and use it. Sometimes it means they say and do some fairly outrageous things. If this is too undisciplined for you, then we should talk pedagogy and philosophy."

My words were met with silent air. Adolfo stood up again, a sign to me that the meeting was soon to be over, and said, "If I hear that anything said in this meeting comes out any place else, I will know where it came from and you will be fired."

I DECIDED NOT TO talk with anyone about my meeting with Adolfo, but my overall look of depression and resignation led Elena to ask me what was happening. She was with Cesar and both wanted to know what was up.

I went into their office, sat down, and spilled my guts. I gave a blow-by-blow description. I finished by saying that what I just said "really has to stay in this room." Both were outraged, but agreed. I trust them, but the walls seem to have ears in this place.

The next morning, I got a call from the receptionist telling me there was a memo in my box and I should pick it up. It was my formal reprimand, entitled, "Re: Work Place Ethics." It said that Adolfo will "not tolerate any unconstructive behaviors" or "any attempt to undermine, embarrass, obstruct or undermine my position as executive director via the spreading of innuendo or falsehood." If I did so, it would result in "immediate termination of employment."

A MONTH LATER, as I was leaving work, I looked into my box and found another memo from Adolfo. It stated that I would no longer be allowed to take winter, spring, or summer breaks. My salary will stay the same so I end up working nearly 3 additional months at the same salary I am making now.

I was livid. Anger. Frustration. I had to figure out some appropriate way to respond. I wrote a memo. At my next meeting with Adolfo and Daniel I purposely positioned myself in the chair next to the south wall of his room to give me more space and not allow him to physically or psychologically box me in like he did last time we met. Daniel sat to my far right with Adolfo between us.

Adolfo began the discussion by telling me he had many problems with my memo. I listened. He held up a copy of the 1988 personnel guidelines and said, "There is nothing in here that says the high school staff have 10-month contracts. I don't know why you say you have a contract since nothing is signed." I explained that when I was hired, the high school staff worked 10-month contracts and, as far as I know, that has always been true. I told him it was unfair to change my status, especially since it means a drastic cut in pay. He said, "The people you should be blaming for this are the sick motherfuckers who were the previous directors and didn't write anything down. You aren't a principal. You're just a teacher and you will be paid like a teacher. A principal is an administrator and should be attending meetings in the evenings. Principals don't teach. You have to choose. Are you a principal or a teacher?"

I answered by telling him I am a teacher of teachers as well as a teacher of students. "I am the one who oversees all aspects of the high school, meets with teachers and students, and represents the school, as well as teaching." I tried to tell him the importance of being immersed within the high school. He responded by saying, once again, "You have to decide whether you are a teacher or an administrator."

"I don't see it as an either-or proposition," I said. "Nobody is going to get paid for 12 months when they only work 10," Adolfo replied. "I don't know what you do. I don't have a job description for you." I told him I'd write one up and give it to him. He said, "I will be the one who decides what you do. I could fire you today and the high school would go on." I said, "That's true, but that doesn't mean it would be right and that there wouldn't be negative consequences." He told me, "The high school would manage fine without you." I sarcastically responded, "The board could fire you today and the agency would go on too."

Adolfo followed by saying, "I want a real high school here." I countered that we are a real high school and many of our students go on to college. He called the high school an "embarrassment" to him. "You have unqualified people teaching and you are not a good disciplinarian." He called the students "fucked up" because he hears too much noise coming from the high school. "They aren't taught to function in the real world," he said. "They need more supervision within the school and you and the teachers are not doing it." If he continues to hear too much noise, or swearing, or if he hears of anything he "disapproves" of, I will receive another written reprimand.

Adolfo continued. "I will decide what is best for the students. Don't forget, I can fire you at any time." I countered by saying, "I fully understood the power dynamics here. It is clear that you are the ultimate authority and have the power to hire and fire." He responded by saying that this is true and that what we talk about "stays between the two of us." Although I knew what he meant, I asked for clarification. He told me I could not talk with the high school staff or I would be fired. I took the tack of explaining to him that the high school is a cooperative, or in his terminology, a "team." As such, I exist within the framework of that team. "I need their input. Especially if there are going to be changes. They need to be involved in that process."

Adolfo looked straight at me and said, "There is only one team at Aztlan Alternative and I am the leader of the team. I will not have you inciting the teachers. If I hear of any protests from them, I will fire all of them all immediately. I know what you're up to in the high school."

There was obviously not much point in continuing this discussion. I told him I had to get back upstairs. I left feeling shell-shocked. These meetings take a toll on me. They confirm in my mind that he wants me and the other staff out of here, but he doesn't yet have grounds to fire us. We need a strategy to preserve what we've built.

24

The Teachers Talk with Adolfo

While I am sitting at my desk writing student evaluations, my phone rings. "This is Mark." It's Daniel. "You should be hearing the news at your meeting with Adolfo this afternoon," he tells me, "but I don't know how you're going to feel about it." "Good news or bad news?" I answered. "It depends." "Just tell me, Daniel." "I'm no longer in charge of the high school for the management team," he said. "Adolfo appointed himself." Out of the frying pan, into the fire. I saw Elena on my way down to my meeting with Adolfo and told her what I'd heard. "I better get my resumé together," she said.

Adolfo started by telling me he chose the best person he knew to head up the high school. "Do the teachers understand that this is not a real high school? Do they understand that if they do not make adjustments, they will lose it all? I want accountability and numbers." He handed me my "new" job description and said, "You will work 12 months. You are not a teacher. I intend to cut the fat around here. No one is going to get paid for not working. Teachers will no longer be paid for not working during the Christmas or spring breaks." I argued again that teachers and I are on 10-month contracts. "The breaks are part of our agreement. You can't cut our pay and treat these as days we don't work."

I might as well have been talking to a dead horse. I started to pack up my briefcase when I told him the high school staff requested he meet with us. He agreed to come to the next staff meeting. "I don't want this to be a kangaroo court," he said. "The teachers have to understand who pays their salaries. I play two roles here. I have my public face as an activist. My other face is I receive my paycheck from the federal government. Do the high school teachers understand this? If they want to debate philosophy I'll do it, but I've already put in my revolutionary experience. If they want to preach their revolutionary doctrine then they should go off to the jungles. If people want to take it out to the alley then that's what I'll do."

As I got up and began to walk to the door, Adolfo said, "I am now requiring you to attend management-team and impact-team meetings. You were supposed to be at this morning's meeting." I replied, "I will comply, but how am I supposed to be at a meeting I don't know about? I was here in the building. Someone could easily have found me." Adolfo turned to his desk, so I left the room.

THE HIGH SCHOOL STAFF asked for this meeting with Adolfo, our first in over 5 months. Cesar and Alexis are proposing we ask him pointed questions. Manuel is biting his tongue. He doesn't agree, but has no alternative to offer. We asked Alberto, as our staff elder, to introduce and facilitate the discussion.

Adolfo positioned himself to the side, away from the teachers. Alberto introduced the discussion. "We need to work for harmony and balance. Today's meeting between the high school and Adolfo is part of a healing process. We need to listen to each other while we air our concerns." Alexis led off the questioning. "Where do you see the high school going from here?"

"I have given the high school enough time to make changes," he said, "and I haven't seen any. All of the curriculum needs to go through me for my approval. I want to see measurable outcomes, a library and computer center, a large child-care center, and I want the school to be more community-oriented. I want the students to be change agents in the community. You should be nurturing and cultivating the youth to be change agents so they can address problems such as drugs, abuse, and marital issues. We need to make students into leaders."

Adolfo looked around the room. It felt like we were listening to a politician. He continued. "I have survived this year and I am looking for people committed to change. I am not trying to be the dictator people say I am. I can be very supportive if there is communication. If you want a pay raise, show me you're worth it."

In a challenge to our dual role as teachers and advisers to students, he asked, "Are you teachers or counselors? You can't be both." Elena said, "You seem to be making assumptions without really knowing what we do." "I only know what I expect and you are not meeting my expectations," he responded. "I gave you people the benefit of the doubt this year to see if you were willing to make changes. One of the things I am going to do is change the job descriptions. I will write them up and give them to you when they are ready. If I had been in the high school as long as some of you I would have changed a lot of things already."

Elena jumped on Adolfo's last comment. "There have been a lot of changes. Just ask Alberto, who has been here the longest. If you never talk with us or come to our meetings, how are you going to know what's even happening in the high school?" Adolfo didn't miss a beat. "If I don't see it, then it's not happening. You teachers need to practice what you preach. I am here to save lives. What are you doing about drugs and abuse? I've told you my door is open. Not one teacher has ever come to talk with me. This agency needs more loyalty."

Robert asked about the hiring process, which historically is done collectively by the teaching staff. Adolfo said, "Now that I have taken over the high school, it is my prerogative to do the hiring." Manuel asked for clarification on "my role as a line staff in the agency." Adolfo turned his chair to face Manuel. "My dream is a barrio where everyone gets along together. Sometimes you have to play with the devil. In fact, I would sell my soul to the devil to save my community. You need to practice what you preach first in your own family and community."

Adolfo then turned to the whole staff, announced that the meeting with him was over, and said, "I don't fall on my knees for any one. My grandmother once said there are lambs and there are lions and the lions eat up the lambs. I learned to never be a follower and to always be a lion."

25

Javier

Today's assembly hosted eight young people visiting from other countries. Part of an international tour, each has experienced violence in his or her life in Ireland, El Salvador, Bosnia, Guatemala, or Cambodia. Following their initial presentations, we broke into smaller groups for discussion.

In one group, a young woman from Ireland spoke of growing up, being expected to hate Protestants, and how she beat up another young woman and got kicked out of school. She ended up going to an integrated school with Protestants and Catholics. She said she is working to break the cycle she found herself in. She asked Aztlan Alternative students to talk about their lives here and how they are impacted by violence. Lilia and Marcel, who are not in gangs but hang out with gang members, talked about how many people they know who have been killed. Lilia said, "I had five friends killed just in the past year and a sixth one just three weeks ago." Marcel talked about "leaving my last school because the neighborhood where I live meant that at school I was associated with the gang from there. I just got tired of getting beaten up."

Their comments brought a quick response from some of the gang members. "Gangs are like a family," said Pablo. "If someone kills someone from your gang you have to strike back. At least two for one." Natalia, who is 7 months pregnant, added, "I have had nine people I know who have died."

Javier motioned to speak and the group calmed to a hush. Javier's physical stature is exceeded only by his rank in his gang. A member since his pre-teens, he is viewed in school as a gang elder and adviser to younger members. "My 14-year-old brother was killed 3 weeks ago by my own boys. I grew up in violence. I've got the marks on my body to show it. I've been busted for shootings and I've been shot at myself. I know I can never forget those three guys who killed my brother." The woman from Ireland pleaded, "Please break the cycle of violence." Javier responded, "This is the only life I know."

JAVIER HAS BEEN my advisee for 3 years. The next morning in advisee group he told me he feels tired. "I'm 20 years old and I feel like I'm 40. I see other people my age and I think about how much more I've experienced than they have. These young guys just coming up, they don't understand." I reminded him of conversations we had when he first came into the school, when he told me being a gangster was his life. "I was young then," he said.

Shortly before Christmas, after students left school on break, I got a call from the receptionist asking if I had heard about Javier's 14-year-old brother being shot last night. I hadn't. She said Javier was coming up the stairs to see me. I met him at the entrance to the library. His eyes were red. His brother was leaving the park district gym when three guys in hooded sweatshirts came up behind him and shot him four times at close range. He died instantly. "It was guys from my own gang who killed him." Javier was close to his brother and wouldn't let him join the gang. "I didn't want him to have to live like me. My mother is taking it real hard. There's going to be a small wake this afternoon and then the body is going to be sent back to Mexico. My father is already there and the rest of the family is leaving today." As he left, we gave each other a hug, something we had not done before.

About 2 weeks after classes started back up, Javier was absent from school for 2 days. I was sitting at my desk about to call him when Marta, Javier's girlfriend and the mother of his 2-year-old son, appeared at my door. "Javier has been arrested for attempted murder," she told me. "He and my sister's cousin were driving down the wrong block when some guys surrounded their car and began throwing bottles. The police say someone in the car started shooting and one guy was hit in the chest three times. He's in critical condition in the hospital. Javier was pulled over. The police say they found a gun under the seat of his car. When they got to the station, two girls identified him as the shooter and he was arrested." Tears welled up in her eyes as Marta said that Javier's family doesn't have the money to bond him out. Javier was on track to be the first person in his family to graduate from high school. I asked about lawyers and Marta said the one that usually represents members of the gang was handling the case. She told me visiting was limited to Fridays. I told her to let him know I would be there this week.

It was bitterly cold as I approached the concertina wire–lined fence and guard station. After a 10-minute wait, during which I felt like my nose was going to fall off, I showed my driver's license and signed in. The male guard came out and told me to raise my arms and spread my legs so he could frisk me. He reentered his warmed concrete hut and pushed a button that allowed the next barbed wire–topped gate to unlock. I walked through, only to wait another 5 minutes until he unlocked the next gate. From here I followed a 200-foot concrete pathway up to another locked door. Buzzed in by an invisible eye, I walked up two flights of metal stairs to another locked door. The eye found me again and buzzed me into a 10- by 20-foot concrete room with three locked doors. One went to the unisex washroom, another to the visiting area, the third to the guard's room. Through a thick glass window, the female guard gruffly asked whom I was here to visit. Before I could answer, she asked if I was carrying any weapons or drugs. Although my impulse was to give a smart-ass answer, I restrained myself and said no. She didn't even look up as she scanned a long computer printout searching for Javier's name. "What is your relationship to the inmate?" she barked. "I'm his high school principal," I told her. She looked up at me. "Okay, go wait by the door."

Once at the visiting-room door, I heard the familiar buzz. I entered yet another concrete room, this one much larger and nearly filled with what looked like mothers, girlfriends, and family members, plus a few small groupings of similarly clad young men and women who looked to be gang members. This process had now taken me over 45 minutes. It would be another 45 minutes before I would see Javier.

The large concrete bricks were painted institutional yellow. I sat on one of the six hard metal benches bolted to the floor. Prisoners are brought down in shifts for their 20-minute visits. Most of the visitors are African American. There were a handful of Latinos and one other white. Probably in his late 20s, thin, and dressed in black, his body language projected discomfort.

Visiting takes place through a 4- by 4-foot piece of well-worn plexiglass. Visitors sit on wooden stools attached to the floor via a 6-inch thick metal cylinder, reminding me of a row of urinals separated by triangular pieces of metal. To talk, you put your mouth up to a dirt-clogged 3-inch hole covered with wire mesh in the center of the plexiglass. To listen, you reverse the process and put your ear to the wire mesh. Eye-to-eye contact is limited to nonverbal communication.

The other white guy and I were called up together and placed next to each other. The visiting cubicles were full. When all the prisoners are present, it is hard to hear even your own conversation. Today, the other white guy's visitor is brought down first, which means most of us can hear them clearly. The prisoner talked of working in films. He said he'd been in jail a month. He described to his friend how he'd been arrested for robbing a small grocery store near where he lived. The friend asked, "Have they charged you with any of the other ones yet?" The prisoner answered, "They haven't put me in any line-ups so I don't think I'll get busted for those." An older black man who was seated next to me looked over. We both shook our heads.

Javier looked good as he stepped up to the cubicle. It was extremely difficult to talk as we took turns leaning into the wire-mesh hole. Javier told me, "I'm only charged with aggravated assault now. They might hit me with some higher charges at the preliminary hearing. The cops only found one gun. They also found an ankle holster on me, but there was no gun in it. I think the guy was shot with a smaller gun than the one they got." I asked him about the two witnesses. "They might be too scared to testify. I got a cousin who's in their gang. I'm hoping they can work out some kind of deal where one of their people gets free in exchange for me. I can also cop to assault and probably just get 2 years. Otherwise I'm looking at 8 to 30. But, if I go to prison, I'll be able to see some guys I haven't seen for awhile."

I asked Javier how things were going inside. "I'm probably going to be here for awhile. My father says he can't bail me out. He thinks I'm safer in here than on the streets. I told him not to worry." He said the gang leadership told him "not to mess with any payback for my brother's killing. They'll deal with the guys who did it." When I asked him if he needed anything, he told me, "You know, I got rank in here. The ones who have it hard are the neutrons [nongang members]. One just got beat up. They get their food taken away from them every day. I want to get some books in so I can teach the other prisoners some of the things I've learned at school about my history."

I told Javier, "If you have to stay in here for awhile, what we can do is try and graduate you straight from jail. We'll hold the graduation ceremony right here in the visiting room if we have to." I brought with me a list of the classes he needs to complete and we worked out a plan. Teachers will write up assignments and I'll arrange to get him books. He can send out his completed work. Javier is also going to write up his own curriculum for a class on Mexican and Indigenous Studies and teach it while in jail.

Our 20 minutes flew by. The guard appeared, tapping each prisoner on the shoulder, announcing that they had to get up immediately. Waiting for buzzing doors, I watched the other visitors as we walked downstairs and across the pathways. There was a solemnness to our procession. For many, this has become a weekly ritual.

I didn't visit Javier again. I learned that he is allowed only one visitor each week. We wrote back and forth and then I didn't hear from him for about a month. Suddenly, he appeared at my office door. "Javier," I shouted. "What's up. It's great to see you. What happened?"

Javier told me that his lawyer arranged a deal in which the two young women wouldn't testify against him in exchange for the brother of a member of his gang not testifying against a member of a rival gang. This meant the state had no case and had to drop charges. After four months in jail, Javier looked good and had in his hand a packet of homework. He told me he had talked with his father and tonight they are going out to buy him a suit to wear to graduation.

Javier completed his schoolwork and arrived at graduation in a dark green suit with his father, his mother, two uncles, Marta, her sister, and his son. He and his parents beamed with joy. As he accepted his diploma, Marta cried as their son held out a bouquet of flowers that Javier graciously held up, along with his son, to the cheers of his family.

26

Danny

The receptionist called up to my office just before lunch and said there were three cops downstairs. They wanted to see Danny. I walked across the hall to the art room to talk with him. Danny didn't know what was up, but said the police had been looking for him at his house last night. His sister answered the door, while he stayed in a back room. I suggested he call his mother at work. She said she'd be over within 10 minutes.

I told Danny we'd stay upstairs until his mother arrived. He saw her park her car, then we met at the entrance to the building. The three of us talked briefly. It was okay with her for Danny to talk with the police as long as she was there. I told her I would arrange for a room and stay with them if she wanted. She said yes. I walked over to the three police, two white, one Mexican, all in plainclothes, wearing jeans, two with flannel shirts, one with a grey sweatshirt, and all three wearing black flak vests. They said they wanted to talk privately with Danny. I told them they could talk to him here as long as both his mother and I were present. They did not object.

As we entered the room, I wanted to talk with Danny and his mother again, but the police started getting pushy and said they were ready to begin. I told Danny and his mother I wanted to clarify that legally they didn't have to talk without a lawyer present. "This is your right and your choice." The taller white cop said they would tell them, but I said I wanted to make sure this was understood by everyone. Danny's mother looked to me, then to the police. She said they would talk.

The shorter white cop stood off to the side. The other two played the Mutt-and-Jeff routine. The tall white cop was the nice cop to the Mexican's mean cop. Their story was that three guys had murdered a fourth two nights ago, stabbing him 18 times. They'd already picked up two of the suspects. They are in jail. The third suspect was on house arrest, but he broke out of his electronic monitoring bracelet and is now a fugitive.

As they began questioning Danny, they called him Frosty. The white cop says, "Okay, Frosty, we think you're the fourth guy." Danny responded that Frosty was not his name. The Mexican cop stepped forward, getting close to Danny. "Don't play with us, Frosty. We know that's your name on the street." The white cop dropped a 5-by-7 picture in his lap. "Do you know this guy?" Even I could tell Danny knew him, but I didn't know how he'd respond. He said yes.

The two cops took turns peppering him with questions about whom he knows and where this guy in the picture could be hiding. I assumed it was the fourth suspect. They implied that Danny was his good friend. Danny told me later that when he got home that night his grandmother described these same three police as the ones who came to his home this morning demanding to search Danny's room. They did not present a search warrant and his grandmother didn't let them in the house.

The good cop asked Danny to give them names. "That's all we want," he kept saying. Danny finally gave them the name of a former girlfriend of one of the guys in jail. The bad cop moved directly in front of Danny's chair. Peering over him and raising his voice, he asked, "Where does she live?" "I don't know," Danny said. The Mexican cop wouldn't back off. "Give me more details." "A brown house, second from the corner, over near the block next to the boulevard," Danny finally offered.

The white cop moved between them and said, "We've got enough." He gave Danny a plain white card with a phone number. "Call us when you want to talk. Remember, talking to us is confidential. Don't tell anyone we were here talking with you." The Mexican cop concluded their interrogation by adding, "We know who you are, Frosty. Call us."

The third cop followed the other two out of the room. The Mexican cop stopped at the pay phone, put in his money, dialed, then kept his hand near the receiver so no one could hear his voice. He was off in less than a minute. Together they walked out the door and straight to their car. Danny, his mother, and I stayed in the room. They were both scared. Danny said he knows who Frosty is. "Frosty don't even look like me." Danny's mother said she is afraid they are trying to set up her son. "I know Danny doesn't always do good, but he doesn't know anything about this." I encouraged them to get in touch with a lawyer.

27

Benito

I lost it with Benito this morning right before first period. Sitting in the student lounge at one of the middle tables, he and two other guys were looking at an infrared miniature flashlight, the kind that is supposed to blind people if you shine it into their eyes. They were laughing as they flashed it up and down into my eyes as I entered the room. Each time it flashed, I asked them not to do it anymore. I was getting irritated, but I didn't say anything. They went off to class. I needed to see Cesar before my class, so I walked down to the science lab. As I turned the corner, I walked right into the red light. I yelled, "Turn it off!" Benito refused, so I walked over and demanded that he give it to me. "You're not listening," I said. "I have asked you too many times already to give it up with the flashlight. It can be dangerous. Now it's mine until after school." Benito didn't want to hand it over, so I took it out of his hand. He jumped up and got in my face. Cesar stood up and stepped between us. I left, telling Benito he could get it back after school.

I know that part of the reason I am so upset with Benito is because of everything else that is happening here. I walked into my class and Johnny saw my face. He said he had never seen me this mad before. "What happened?" I told him and the other students in the room. "You want me to go stick him?" Johnny offered. I said no, and wrote the words discipline and self-discipline on the board. "What's the difference?" I asked the class. Roberto responded that discipline is "getting whacked for something you did wrong." I explained that discipline stems from self-discipline. "Self-discipline should be the essence of what our school is all about. That was violated today by Benito and by me."

After class I went into the science lab to find Benito and Cesar. I apologized for going off on Benito and explained to him why I was upset. "It's the disrespect that bothers me most, Benito. And then you get in my face like I'm the one who flashed the red light at you." Cesar is Benito's adviser and used this incident to talk with him about his schoolwork. "What's up?" he asked him. "You've been faking it off in my class and then lying to me about having done work in your small group." Benito said, "That's not true." "I saw you," responded Cesar. "And this is going on in almost every class." Benito, who is about five foot four with a clean-shaven head except for one long lock hanging off to the side, kept up his veneer of toughness until Cesar told him that if he didn't start doing work in class, he wouldn't earn his credit. "I know this stuff already," Benito said. Although Cesar does not believe that to be true, he asked Benito to work with him in presenting tomorrow's lesson. Benito seemed reluctant, but agreed to talk with Cesar after school. We all shook hands as we walked off to our next classes.

28

Maria Elena

Maria Elena's mother has always been supportive of the school. She tells us that this is the best place for her daughter. "Now she has a chance to graduate from high school and do something for herself and her child." Unfortunately, Maria Elena has not done well academically. She wanders the halls, does little homework, and tends to spend most of her time talking with other students in class. She says she loves being in school and I believe her. She has a great social life here and brings her daughter to child care every day. We've had numerous discussions with her, finally voting as a staff to ask her to sit out one session. She can come back and give it another try in the fall.

The afternoon after we told Maria Elena, I got a call from her mother. She is mad that we are not "letting my daughter back into school." I tried to explain to her the process we went through and how Maria Elena had been a part of it each step of the way. "She knew the consequences of her actions," I told her. Then she tells me, "The most unfair thing is that Maria Elena already told her case worker she will be in school and now she won't receive her benefits if it isn't true." I tried to be empathetic and explain that we understand, but we also don't keep students in school in order to meet someone else's requirements, such as probation or state aid. "The issue is Maria Elena's performance in school. We discussed it fully in our staff meeting and everyone agreed to ask her to sit out until fall. She can petition to return earlier, but I can't guarantee it will meet with staff approval." Maria Elena's mother started yelling at me. "You don't care about kids. You're not even willing to give my daughter a second chance." Even as I tried to explain to her that Maria Elena has had numerous second chances, she got madder, repeatedly interrupting me, and finally hung up. I'm confident we tried our best and made a correct decision with Maria Elena, but I still feel bad, real bad.

29

The Smoking Lounge

I called for an emergency assembly right after first period. Only a couple staff knew what was up. I brought in some of the artifacts from last night—a burnt battery, a burnt plastic lighter, and a burnt piece of wood. "I walked into the student lounge about 4:30 yesterday," I told the group. "I wanted to make sure it was clean and presentable for the board meeting. What did I find? Black and grey ashes scattered everywhere. Then I walked into the smoking room." I brought out the evidence. It was greeted with amazement and a few groans. "It took me nearly an hour to get this place back together. With the smoking lounge, I just shut the door and put a sign on it saying it was closed. But what really bothers me is wondering what was going on with the students who obviously were having some kind of fire going on in the smoking room. What's up? This is serious and I'm presenting it back to you. I'd like the students who did it to come forward and explain why. Then we need to come up with a plan for consequences."

I was met with choruses of "I didn't do it; I wasn't here yesterday; we don't know anything." "Well," I said, "someone knows something. This is something we all need to take responsibility for." A voice from the back called out. "I did it. I'll clean it up." It was Leonard, someone I would not have suspected. "We were just playing," he said. "It got out of hand." "What do you think we should do?" I asked. "I'll clean it up," he offered. Selina spoke up. "What about you, Eddie?" Eddie gave her a stare and said, "What are you picking on me for, girl?" "You know you were there with Leonard," she said. Other students joined in. Finally, Eddie agreed to help and their other partner, Tony, also spoke up and "volunteered" to be part of the clean-up.

Alexis stood up and said she knew what had happened but hadn't said anything. I was surprised she knew. She said she was wrong not to say anything. I offered up a proposal that the smoking lounge be temporarily closed, but some students objected that it wasn't fair to punish everyone. I asked if they would accept its being closed until it was cleaned and repainted and they agreed.

30

Getting High at Lunch

I got a call from the receptionist telling me she heard six students were seen smoking marijuana in the new, unfinished child-care room. Immediately after I hung up I got a call from the head of the business office ordering me to come upstairs. He asked me to sit down and, in a stern voice, said, "We have a crisis." I played dumb and asked what he meant. He told me that one of the child-care workers saw six guys walking out of the room next door. When she investigated, the room smelled of marijuana. "I've already told Adolfo," he said. "They need to be dropped from the high school. Are you going to have them arrested?" I told him I needed to talk with the suspected students and then "I'll take care of it."

Just what we didn't need. As I walked back downstairs and into the student lounge, who should I find but five of the six students. I said, "We need to talk, guys. We've got a big problem. I want to get straight what just happened over in the new child-care room. It feels like they're out for blood on this one. Be honest with me and I'll do what I can to help resolve it and keep you in school." They feigned that they didn't know what was up. "It's about smoking weed next door," I said. Jason said he didn't know what I was talking about. "Get off it guys," I answered. I was getting mad now. "You've got to deal with this one. You were seen walking out of the room by other people in the building. This is my head as well as yours." They kept denying they did anything and told me it wasn't fair of me to accuse them. Everyone seemed to be talking at once. I yelled out, "Don't give me this shit. I don't need it and you don't need it. We don't have time to play around. If you don't cop to it then we're going to have no choice but to ask you to leave school. If you want to get real and talk and deal with the consequences, you have 5 minutes to come upstairs to Elena's office."

I walked out of the lounge and up the stairs. Elena had a group of students in her room doing beading. They could tell I was upset and asked me what was happening. I told them, since I knew it would be around school soon anyway. Javier was there and said they "need to face the consequences because this could jeopardize the whole school." In less than 5 minutes, all five showed up at Elena's door. I let them talk in front of the other students. They said they smoked in the alley, not the building, and that it couldn't have smelled as bad as everyone said. "Either way," I said, "it's already all over the building and we need to figure out a process to try and get out of this or all of us are in trouble." I also said I needed to know who the other person was. They wouldn't say, so I tried to guess, allowing them not to snitch, but giving them the chance to verify my guess. It didn't take long because I knew who hung out with them.

My first proposal was immediate suspension, a written apology, and next week they come in with individual written statements for their advisers addressing their participation and why they want to be back in school. Just as I told them, "even this is no guarantee because I don't know what the administration is going to want," I got a call to go to Adolfo's office. His secretary said he wanted to know what I was going to do. In his office, I took a chance and went for his ego. "How about if you talk to them, Adolfo? They're all gang members who are trying to make it in school. They admit they made a mistake. You talk with them." The look on his face changed. He agreed.

I went upstairs and asked the students if they would be willing to talk to Adolfo. "Tell him you were wrong. You're coming forward because you know this could hurt the school. You want to make things better and try and be back in school." They were hesitant, but I didn't give them much of a choice. I figured having to talk with Adolfo was apt punishment. Jason looked worried. He'd be high in Adolfo's office. Javier told him, "You'll lose your high quick when you get in the room with him." I led them downstairs, cautioning them not to giggle.

About 20 minutes later they arrived back upstairs. "He was straight," said Jason. "He told us how he was just like us. He grew up in the barrio and got high with his boys. He told us not to get high here in school." That was it. I apologized to them for getting mad. Jason said it was okay. "You were just trying to do what you thought was best." We walked outside together. I told them they still needed to come in Monday with written statements and talk with their advisers before being able to come back to classes. They joked that I was being too hard on them as they took off down the boulevard.

31

Flaco

A few minutes after school started, I headed down the stairs and saw Flaco walking in late, wearing a scarf with his gang colors. I was never sure why he was called Flaco because he looked more like an offensive guard on a football team. "Flaco, you've got to put that in your locker," I said as I passed him going up the stairs. "Fuck you," he told me. I wasn't in the mood to deal with him today so I asked Patrice, his adviser, to talk with him. Flaco's got a tough demeanor, but he's never sworn at me before. She agreed and I went up to his class to send him back down to see her.

As I entered the room, the chairs were set up in a circle and Flaco was closest to the door. I softly put my hand on his shoulder to get his attention. He forcefully pushed it off. I apologized for touching him and told him he needed to go see Patrice. He stood up, inches from my face, and spat out, "Fuck you." For the first time ever at Aztlan Alternative I thought a student might take a punch at me. I knew I would just take it, but I was angry. The room stood silent for what seemed an eternity. Flaco finally walked around me and out the door. I heard later from Patrice that she also thought he was so angry he could have hit her when he was in her office. Flaco's not one to communicate verbally and Patrice never did find out what was bothering him, although she felt it was something outside of school.

After Flaco left the room, I stood there looking at the class and at Manuel, the teacher. Then I went off. I was surprised at how angry and upset I was and I asked them, both the students and Manuel, why they didn't do anything about Flaco's blatantly wearing his colors. "What makes the no-representing rule work is everyone enforcing it, not just leaving it up to me or Patrice." No one responded, so I left.

About 2 months later I was washing out my coffee pot in the third-floor bathroom when I noticed two young guys I did not know looking through the small window in the fire door that separates the hallways from the stairway. I walked out to see what was up. One was about five foot nine, the other about half a foot shorter, and both were slim. As I approached them they represented at me with their hands. "What's up guys?" I asked. "We're looking for someone," the shorter one responded. I asked who and they didn't answer. I told them they had to leave the building and tried to escort them down the stairs. As we approached the first landing the taller guy yelled out the name of their gang and said they were members. "I know," I replied.

As we reached the second-floor door, they tried to enter a classroom. I told them again they had to leave the building. The taller one said, "No one tells us what to do." "It's school rules," I said. The shorter one called me out. "You're a punk, man. When you want to box it out?" Foolishly, I said, "Anytime." Fortunately, they kept walking and left the building. As I started back up the stairs, Flaco met me and said he'd heard what happened. "I'll get them for you," he told me and started racing down the stairs. I was surprised by his response, but I asked him to come back. He did. We looked at each other for a moment, then Flaco walked into class, his gruff mask back on his face.

32

The Impact and Management Teams

The idea behind the impact team is to create an agency leadership group comprised of the management team and middle-level managers. In practice, it looked to me to be an attempt to create a group of docile lieutenants who would implement policy handed down by Adolfo and Alfredo. I felt sickened by the process, but knew I needed to attend to keep my job and to continue to be a buffer between Adolfo and the high school.

Our initial meeting lasted 3 hours. We sat around in a horseshoe with Alfredo standing up front. He lectured us on assessment and presented an "evaluation tool" we are expected to take back to our units. It looked like a sophisticated football betting sheet. We did a walk-through in which Alfredo ran down what each number in the evaluation grid stood for and its relationship to every other number. Everyone agreed to do it on themselves and bring the results to the next meeting. I brought it to a high school staff meeting. I felt like a stand-up comic. It is hard to take it seriously, it is so inimical to our philosophy and practice.

The next three impact-team meetings were a circus. I really tried my best to be a good employee. This all feels so fake. I'm the only one who raises any questions or concerns. But I try to be on my best behavior. Outside the meeting, I hear criticisms and questions, but no one seems willing to say anything in the meetings.

The impact-team meetings have become the low point of my days. The stress and tension are wreaking havoc on my back and neck. I try deep breathing before I enter the room, but what little relaxation I achieve never lasts more than 15 minutes. It leads to a pounding headache that reaches the point where my head feels like it is going to burst.

Alfredo is clearly the leader of this process. Even he is beginning to get frustrated. One night he asked us, "What is this group's purpose? It will not work unless we all agree on its purpose." He was met with silence. He told us, "Speak your minds and brainstorm." More silence. I took a chance and said, "A quality program that meets peoples' needs and serves as a model to other programs is a good purpose." Some of the other staff liked this idea, but Alfredo jumped on me quickly. He told us our purpose: "Zero defects." Martín, a member of the management team, made the mistake of asking, "What if someone does not agree?" Adolfo, who is conspicuously silent in these meetings, stood up, pointed his finger at Martín and said, "I will make sure that anyone who does not agree will no longer be working at Aztlan Alternative."

At the next meeting, Alfredo told us we needed to address a series of questions. What do we do about people who are not here? I had become one of the few middle managers who attended regularly. The initial round of suggestions recommended docking pay. Someone else proposed one allowable, excused absence. A concern was raised about legitimate absences, like sickness. Alfredo and Adolfo remained silent.

"Zero defects" was again the correct answer. No absences. Attendance must be mandatory. I decided to raise the issue of sickness and said, "Invariably, people get sick or have family emergencies so there needs to be a level of trust. If someone needs to be absent, this should be possible." Alfredo responded, "This is not an issue of trust. We have to decide what standards are acceptable."

Alfredo went on to the second question. "We must ask ourselves why are we here, what are we willing to contribute, and is my participation essential?" Everyone was told to answer. Alfredo wrote our responses on large sheets of butcher paper taped to the wall. After we spoke, Alfredo gave us titles. There was the "doubter," the "new voice," the "doer." I was the "initiator." It felt like Snow White and the Seven Dwarfs.

Alfredo posed the next question: Do any of us believe the agency is in a crisis? Before we could answer, Adolfo offered another question. Why is no one doing anything about the crisis? Since the assumption is that none of us either recognize it or are doing anything, our collective response was silence. Adolfo launched into a diatribe about how we are all perpetuating our "dysfunctional view that someone else will fix our problems for us." This, of course, led us to the next point. Alfredo and Adolfo are willing to lead us, but we have to agree we are dysfunctional and we need their guidance and help. Who could disagree when the choice is agreement or termination of employment?

That settled, the issue became what "value discipline" we will embrace to deal with our crisis. Alfredo told us there are three, and only three, possible choices—operational excellence, product leadership, and customer intimacy. We had to choose one as our priority and de-

cide on our "service niche." Wal-Mart and Hertz were given as examples of operational excellence. Alfredo said, "When I pass a Wal-
Mart, I stop and go in just to see how well they do their operations."

Without any discussion, it was made clear that operational excellence and "streamlining" would be the value discipline we adopt. Alfredo said, "We need to discuss this new paradigm more. It would be
good if there was some conflict because conflict pushes a group forward." I decided, what the hell, and jumped in. Before I could even
complete a thought questioning this approach and the chosen discipline, Adolfo cut me off. "There is a crisis here and we're wasting time.
I am ready to fire three or four people and lay off three or four more so
the message gets across that this crisis is real." As an example of how
we should take this seriously, Alfredo said, "Just the other day I was
ready to fire our business manager on the spot. She is a member of our
management team. She proposed we hire two more accounting assis-
tants. I was so mad at her for making that suggestion I wanted to fire
her immediately. She should know there is this new paradigm and
there is no way we could even consider hiring two new people. I was
livid with anger. It was a good thing she had a diabetic attack and had
to go to the hospital because I would have fired her."

Alfredo followed up his story by surveying the group. I was the
only one who did not agree on operational excellence as our value discipline. I asked when we were going to talk about the quality of our
programs. Adolfo asked me if I'd read Lee Iacocca's book. When I said
no, he said, "Quality begins with the managers believing in it." I reminded him that we are a not-for-profit agency, not Chrysler. Adolfo
shot back, "We are about saving lives, not making profits."

PHASE ONE of the impact team's life ended. No announcement, it just
faded away. It reconstituted itself as the management team plus myself
and another middle manager. We meet bi-weekly in the back of the
building, next to the business office.

Alfredo started tonight's session by declaring, "Now that you have
decided operational excellence is the value discipline you agree to
work for, we need to agree on the product we are targeting to the marketplace. What value do the customers care about? Who are our customers?" He started a list on the blackboard and broke it into three
groups: clients, funders, and other agencies. Alfredo proposed a customer survey based on a 0–5 scale. Selected customers will be given a
confidential survey. The results will be recorded and distributed. "This
will expose a lot of flaws in the agency." Adolfo added, "The reason we
should do this is because I already know the answers. People are telling

me negative things when I meet them outside of here. You need to hear it for yourselves."

I kept my mouth shut and listened as Alfredo went on to say, "Depending on the results of the survey, you may have to change your customer base." I wasn't sure what he meant until he said "funders drive the customer base. They drive the company." He used the analogy of Wal-Mart and Nordstrom. "They don't compete with each other's niches in the marketplace. We need to blow our competitors out of the water."

Getting practical, Alfredo said this means "you will have to put more money into administration to provide effective, seamless service." We watched a video on team building. A middle-aged white male executive narrated clips from *The Wizard of Oz*. He explained how Dorothy, the straw man, the tin man, and the lion could not have accomplished what they did without teamwork. He stressed having a mutually agreed upon goal, cooperation, mutual support, small successes to reinforce commitment to each other, openness and honesty, and a common purpose that benefits all.

Alfredo asked, "What do each of you want out of this process?" Before anyone could answer, Adolfo added, "You have to buy a place at the table before being able to voice your opinions and this means honoring your commitments. You have to buy into the process." He made reference to a book he read on excellence in corporations. I made the point, again, that we are not-for-profit. Alfredo responded with "It doesn't matter anymore because there shouldn't be any difference between the two, for-profit and not-for-profit."

33

Can We Save the School?

Sitting around the tables in the library, we stare blankly at each other. Up on the blackboard are the words "Can we save the school?" There is a pervasive feeling that we're just sitting back, watching the school crumble, and not doing much to combat it. Adolfo has us paralyzed. Manuel breaks the silence by suggesting that we mobilize parents. "We could have a community meeting where we discuss the future of the high school and invite the administration. This is bigger than us. Adolfo wants a clean slate. They don't want us around here." I added, "I think they want to use the traditions and reputation of the high school, but they can't afford, from their point of view, to have the kind of program we've developed where teachers, students, and parents have a voice is what's going on."

Alberto asks to speak. "It is frustrating hearing the kinds of speculation everyone is doing. We don't really know what Adolfo wants or what he's planning." "I don't know," I told Alberto. "I think we do know some of what he's doing and if we don't do something soon, he'll just implement his plans after we're gone for the summer, then it's good-bye high school."

"Where do you want to take this, Mark?" asked Manuel. "I'll go as far as we need to go," I answered. "Adolfo is out to destroy this school. I'm ready for whatever it takes to blow it open. I just don't know what that is. After my last meetings with him and my meetings with the impact and management teams, I'm even more convinced I'm dead meat as far as Adolfo is concerned. The only thing that will save me is if we get rid of him. You're going to have to decide what each of you wants to do. I don't think people should put their jobs in jeopardy because of what happens to me. We need some kind of leverage, something we can use to create a crack or a wedge. What we're doing now feels like slow death."

AT OUR NEXT STAFF MEETING, we decided to talk about the school to give ourselves some perspective. We need an honest assessment of the high school. We need to take a look at what kind of core staff would be needed for next year and see who wants to stay. We asked ourselves: Can we come up with a plan that will meet Adolfo's needs as well as our own? This could be moot depending on Adolfo's determination to restructure the high school, but we want to be more proactive and set some of our own terms. One way to begin is to look at ourselves.

Where are we as a school? Cesar said our strengths lie in "the trust, communication, and collaboration among the staff." I concurred. "Student democracy and freedom of expression for students and teachers contribute to this trust."

Manuel suggested that we talk about some of our personal visions as teachers. He began by saying, "I let students vent their frustrations and then I try to help them look for positive solutions." Alexis gave an example from her Algebra II class. "We talked about the content in Algebra II, but they didn't know the material. The students asked that we begin with a review of algebra and now they are studying and paying attention better than ever before." Elena talked about her Spanish as a Second Language class. "Most of them think they don't know much of the language, but once they begin sharing knowledge and information about Spanish, they get excited about how much they already know and understand." I added that one of the things visitors notice right away is how much cooperation and sharing there is among the students.

Other points to come out were that we advise students academically and push for higher education, classes are small, we help students get jobs while they're in school, we have respect for students, we offer tutoring, we have all-school assemblies, there is student involvement in setting up and evaluating the curriculum, we are flexible, and the staff works as a cooperative and not in a hierarchical structure.

Elena made the point that we "establish reasons for why students are studying what they are studying. There is a purpose in their being here and receiving this type of education." Cesar gave the example of how we follow up with students: "We don't leave them hanging. They don't see that in too many parts of their lives."

Not to be too laudatory, Manuel suggested that even though we are a small school, "we are still too big to defend. We have been unable to manage the high school, especially around the paperwork. That's one of Adolfo's biggest complaints: We don't produce the numbers he wants. I think each of us needs to say if we are coming back. Who's not? Everyone should say what they really feel about staying with this ship or giving it up." Manuel led the way and told us he is definitely moving out of state and won't be back. Cesar and Alexis both say they want to be here. They have a commitment to the community and the students and want to see it through. I said I want to be here, but I don't expect I'll be given that chance. Alberto said he will continue to be part of the school. Elena spoke of her 4 years here and how on good days she wants to be here, but on bad days she doesn't even feel like coming in. She does not want to go on a 12-month schedule, as Adolfo has proposed, and lose Christmas and spring breaks with no increase in salary. Angel said, "I'm new here, but I like it so far. I still don't understand why the administration is so hard on the school or why they want cutbacks. We have so little supplies anyway." There was silence while we waited for Robert. He seemed defensive as he told us, "I haven't made up my mind yet. I've been here a long time and I'm not sure what I'm going to be doing next year."

MANUEL AND I are outside the school waiting for the *paleta* man to walk down the sidewalk. "It's time to abandon ship," he tells me. "It's time to bail out. But we shouldn't do it until the end of August, right before school is suppose to begin. We do it all at once and really screw him up. My advice to Cesar and Alexis is to get a 9-to-5 and then come back and have a GED program in the evenings for the students. This way they won't have to deal with neocolonials like Adolfo or funders. It's time to abandon social service agencies. They corrupt you." "What about the two dozen students ready to graduate next year?" I ask him. "They need a viable alternative that won't be there if everyone leaves." "They go to the evening GED program," he replies.

I had to get back upstairs and finally gave up on getting a *paleta*. When you really want one they're never here and other times their pushcarts are bumping into each other. Manuel and I debated brands and I told him my favorite. As I reentered the building I heard the tingling of a *paleta* bell down the block. About 10 minutes later Manuel came up with his mango *paleta* in his hand and told me I gave up too soon. I made a sarcastic comment about how he didn't even get me one. From behind his back he pulled out a *coco de agua*, my favorite.

Munching on my *paleta* as I walk down the stairs, I run into Cesar. "Alexis and I were talking and she has a good idea. I'll lay it out at the staff meeting. What she is proposing is you, representing the high school staff, ask Adolfo to come meet with us one more time. We ask him explicitly what his plans are for the high school." Robert and Elena joined our conversation. Robert asked, "What's the point? He won't listen to us anyway." Elena agreed, but said she would give it a chance.

I was won over to giving it a shot too because I believe Cesar and Alexis really want to stay. So do Elena and Alberto. It will at least give those who want to try an opportunity to hear directly what he is going to say and then make a decision about whether they feel they can work on his terms next year.

Later that afternoon at our staff meeting, Alberto told us, "We need to figure out ways to negotiate through this. This needs to be a time of healing. I want to propose that all of us, the whole high school staff, go to a sweat. It is a spiritual and cleansing experience. We will grow together through the four doors, losing our individuality and growing collectively. It can be a life-changing experience." There was silence. Elena spoke in favor, but no one else said a word. Alberto asked for a show of hands. We decided to do the sweat as a teacher in-service.

34

The Sweat

We all agreed to meet at school and leave by 9:00. We didn't take off until 9:45 and then we left without Angel. We saw him riding his bike and stopped. He locked his old Schwinn to a street sign. Packed into Elena's van and Manuel's car, we headed off to the countryside.

Traveling along the freeways, it took about 50 minutes to get to the small town where the sweat lodge is located. It turned out to be in a housing development, probably from the early 70s. The homes looked weathered and it seemed to be predominantly white with a mix of Latino families. As we approached, Alberto looked around and said "It's a red house. I've been here twice before, but I don't remember where we turn." We circled in and out of cul-de-sacs for another 20 minutes. It seemed as though we'd been in each one at least twice when we decided to leave the development and find a phone as we wandered down one last cul-de-sac. Spotting a rainbow flag, Alberto yelled, "Stop. This is the place."

A split-level suburban home was not my vision of where I would do my first Native sweat, but Alberto assured us they have many ceremonies here. As we parked, Austin walked down the front steps. A large man about 35 with long dark hair tied in a ponytail, he greeted Alberto with a hug. Alberto told us he'd called Austin last night and been assured everything would be ready to go when we arrived. "I'll get the rocks and the fire going," he told Alberto. "Nothing's going yet. I'm sorry but, you know, I'm running on Indian time."

It was a pleasantly warm day, with temperatures near 80°. Although Alberto had told us we'd be out of here by 2:00, we knew we might as well settle in, not expecting to leave before 5:00. Austin led us to the backyard, where we discovered half an acre of land connected on two sides and at the far end with eight other backyards in a circular pattern. In the middle of Austin's yard stood a leafy tree and the sweat lodge, visible to all the other lots.

The sweat lodge was smaller than I expected, maybe 8 feet across and 4 feet high at its peak. The frame was constructed of tree branches strung together like braids and molded into the shape of a geodesic dome. The branches were covered with layers of old military tarps. At the north end was a small door leading out to a 6-foot-long path that ends at a 4-foot-wide and 3-foot-deep pit. Next to the pit was a mound of grey rocks, each about 6 to 8 inches in diameter. Austin said they collect the rocks from a nearby river bed. Behind the rocks lies a wood-pile. Austin asked us to carry over wood for the fire, which he laid across the bottom of the pit on top of crumpled newspaper. At what seemed to me to be random moments, he and Alberto stopped and chanted Native prayers.

After the bottom of the pit was covered with nearly a foot of wood, Austin began placing in layers of rocks. He asked us to gather around and explained that from this point on we should not cross the path from the pit to the sweat lodge. He lit the newspaper. As it began to burn, he handed us handfuls of sage and pine needles to toss on top of the rocks.

It took over an hour and a half for the fire to heat the rocks. As we sunbathed and talked, waiting in anticipation, we were startled by an explosion. We jumped back, then walked up near the pit. Austin explained that since the rocks come from the river they sometimes still have water in them, which causes them to explode. As he was explaining this to us, another rock exploded, sending wood and rock out nearly 10 feet. That was enough to keep me permanently away from the fire.

Austin motioned for Alberto and announced that the rocks were ready. It was then we learned the sweat was going to be led by two Native elders from Wyoming who are visiting Austin's family. A married couple in their late 60s or early 70s, they walked up slowly from the house and sat on lawn chairs at the entrance to the sweat lodge. We had previously been told that normally sweats are done naked, but in situations like ours, it is okay for men to wear shorts or bathing suits and women to wear shorts with T-shirts, light dresses, or bathing suits.

Austin asked us to gather together at the sweat door. "It is an honor today to have with us Leonard and Carolyn," he told us. "They have traveled many miles to be with us. When I told them about your school and your purpose here today, they offered to lead the sweat. I hope you understand what an honor this is." He turned to Leonard. "My father, welcome. We are humbled to have you with us and we appreciate your taking the time to convene this sacred ceremony." Austin opened a wooden case and handed an eagle feather to Leonard. Carolyn held out a bowl filled with sage. Austin lit the sage and Leonard said a prayer in his native language. The bowl was passed to each of us. We held it in front of our chests and fanned the smoke up to our faces with our free hands.

When the bowl returned to Leonard, he spoke in a quiet manner, telling us, "The women will enter first, followed by the men. Myself and Alberto will sit by the opening." He explained that everything moves around the circle in a clockwise direction. "There are four doors. At the beginning of each door, we place rocks in the pit in the center of the sweat. Austin will remain outside, bringing us rocks. He will close the opening when we are ready. After each door, which represent the four directions, we add more rocks. Are you ready to begin?" We looked at each other like innocent children. We nodded that we were ready.

Carolyn led the women in first. The men followed. Alberto sat on the men's side near the opening. Leonard entered last and sat next to his wife. Inside the sweat, we found a small pit in the middle. About a foot deep and 2 feet wide, it left us only 3 feet between it and the edge of the tarp to sit. We scrunched next to each other on the dirt floor. The only covering was occasional 18-inch-square pieces of old carpeting. Skin to skin and half naked, we tried to get as comfortable as possible as we waited to begin the ceremony. Next to Alberto sat Angel, Robert, me, Manuel, Cesar, Elena, Alexis, Carolyn, and Leonard. We were told we could bring in a towel. With the exception of the elders and Alberto, each of us held a towel in our laps. The sweat was about to begin.

Austin brought the first six rocks up one by one on a shovel. Steam rose from the pit as the rocks were placed down. The sweat immediately got hotter. Two of the rocks cracked as they hit other rocks, revealing red hot sparks. The only other objects in the sweat were a small drum, an eagle feather, and a large plastic bucket with an animal horn for taking out water. Alberto filled the horn and splashed the rocks, filling the sweat with steam. Austin closed the door, making the area so dark I could not even see my hand in front of my face. I felt claustrophobic. Leonard sang a native-language song accompanied by Alberto on the drum. Leonard spoke. "We will now go around the circle. Each of you will say a prayer. Alberto, you begin."

As Alberto talked, Carolyn intermittently filled the horn and splashed water on the rocks. The enclosed sweat got hotter and hotter. It was difficult to breathe. Alberto sang two songs in Lakota and prayed for the staff. "This is a time of healing and unity." He ended with a prayer for me, saying he knew it had been a difficult year. Angel followed with a short prayer in Spanish and then Robert spoke of his 6 years at Aztlan Alternative and his hope that we can still save the school.

In the dark and the heat I was beginning to lose track of time. My chest felt tight. My body was covered with sweat, as were Robert's and Manuel's as we rubbed against each other. I was next. "I want to remember four people who are no longer alive who have helped me in my life." I spoke briefly about Bo and Fanon, who befriended me in prison, and my mother and father. As I finished, Leonard called to Austin, who opened the sweat.

We completed the first door. Those of us from the staff expressed relief and joked about the heat. We were already wasted. Alberto filled the horn with water. You are allowed to take what you need, then pass it around the circle clockwise until everyone has their fill. A light breeze passed through the sweat. Leonard told us that there is no shame in leaving before the completion of the four doors, although the only time it is permissible is when the sweat is open. Robert said he needed to leave. He was hyperventilating and did not feel comfortable in the dark and the heat.

I wasn't feeling great myself. My stomach was queasy, but I thought I could continue. The water horn continued around the circle as Angel and Manuel both received gentle reprimands for taking drinks out of turn. Leonard and Carolyn gave us plenty of time before starting the second door.

Austin brought in six more rocks, one by one, to be placed on top of the first six already in the pit. He asked Leonard for permission to sing a song outside after closing up. Carolyn splashed water on the new and old rocks as Austin sang. He was followed by Leonard, who sang a series of songs and said more prayers. He asked us to begin where we left off in the circle. Manuel spoke, followed by Cesar, Elena, and Alexis. My chest felt like it was going to burst. My stomach churned. I knew I was close to vomiting and momentarily thought about how embarrassing that would be. Alberto picked up after Alexis and sang another song while beating on the drum. Throughout this door, Carolyn continually splashed water on the rocks. Finally, Leonard called out to Austin.

As the water horn came to me I spilled it over my chest trying to get it up to my mouth. I seriously considered leaving until Leonard waved the large eagle feather creating a breeze and Carolyn gave a pep talk telling us how proud she was that we made it this far. We all stayed as Austin brought in six more hot rocks.

My recollection of the sequence of events becomes hazy at this point. During the third door, each of us spontaneously began chanting or moaning like ancient monks. This door was shorter than the others. I did not feel as dehydrated and my breathing felt better. Cesar and Elena left after the sweat door opened. Four months pregnant, Elena said she had stopped sweating. Their exit was a blur to me as I slumped into a semi-fetal position, gently rocking back and forth. I told myself that having made it this far I should be able to continue. Alberto gave us lots of encouragement to stay through all four doors. I was feeling good, in a sort of spiritual zone, a kind of natural high that enveloped me as the last six rocks appeared in the pit and the opening closed. The feeling was short-lived.

Carolyn asked to begin and said she would be doing six horns. On either side of me, Angel and Manuel were now lying on the dirt. I continued in my rocking slump. The floor was muddy. My feet slipped whenever I attempted to move. I tried to keep them away from the hot pit. Carolyn tossed on two horns of water. The steam rose up in my face. She said a prayer, sang a song, tossed another horn on the rocks. My face burned and I covered my legs with my towel. I moaned louder and louder although I could hardly hear myself over the other groans and prayers. I vaguely remember Carolyn's talking about the necessity for sacrifice and how suffering is part of the ritual of the sweat.

The fourth door seemed to go on forever. Carolyn sang. Alberto sang. Another horn was tossed on the rocks. Leonard sang. Our moaning filled the small space. Carolyn dropped sage on the rocks and the final horns. Each time she poured on another horn, I rocked in my fetal position, pulling my towel over my head, even though it was soaking wet. My whole body burned. My chanting became a chorus of "nò, no, no" interspersed with something that sounded like "ommm."

Carolyn finished the six horns. My heart raced. The steam seemed to pierce into my bones. Time stopped. I heard a huge splash as the water from the bucket was tossed onto the rocks. Steam came from every direction. I couldn't move. I could barely breathe. When was this going to end? I peeked out from behind the towel to see if there was light. I was melting. I couldn't go on another moment.

Light. There was light. I let the towel fall to my lap. The fourth door was over. Relief. Joy. Misery. Happiness. When it came my turn to leave the sweat my body wouldn't move. Angel, Alberto, and I were the only ones left inside. Alberto said, "It's time to get out." I fell down to my hands and knees. I crawled clockwise around the pit. As I exited the opening, I continued to crawl to the shade of the tree. I collapsed on my back. I'd made it. I couldn't speak. My heart continued to race.

A cloud eventually seemed to lift and life returned to my body. I asked for help and Robert and Alexis gave me their hands. I sat up.

Alberto called us over to the pathway in front of the sweat. We sat in a circle with Austin, Leonard, and Carolyn. Leonard lit a ceremonial pipe. We passed it around, each of us taking puffs. It had a sweet tobacco taste.

Leonard thanked us. He said all of us had done well. He was proud that we persevered. He will pray for our school. Alberto spoke about using today's experience as a healing. Physically, it had been exhausting, but there was a different feeling among us. We smiled and hugged. As we changed clothes and headed back to the city, I kept thinking how I had never been to a teacher in-service like this one.

35

Final Days

We gathered in the student lounge for our last Wednesday assembly. The mood was somber, more like a wake than the usual jubilation of last classes and graduation. It's over. We know we have lost. There are more meetings scheduled with Adolfo, but I hold little hope that they will be successful. On Monday, Adolfo gave me my ultimatum—accept his terms or be terminated. Reluctantly, I decided to resign rather than give him the satisfaction of firing me.

We have a fiesta planned following the assembly. The weather bypassed spring this year. It's already hot and humid. We'll have the festivities outside. Javier has the barbecue set up and he's roasting half a pig. For now, we are packed together, no one wanting to be the first to say the last rites.

We introduce this year's graduates for their final words. Each is positive about experiences here and critical of the new administration. We present them with flowers and go over last-minute graduation plans for this Saturday. We have all the windows open, but little breeze makes its way across the room.

Manuel is the first to speak from the teachers. "I'm going to miss everyone. You, the students, are the ones who are going to have to carry on the school's traditions. I've only been here 2 years, but it's been 2 of the most important years of my life." He started to name students he had worked with and broke down crying. Standing near the smoking room, he quickly walked out to regain his composure.

Robert spoke up next. He told us about his first days at Aztlan Alternative. He doesn't know yet what he is going to do next, but he knows he can't work under the new administration. It's time to move on. Robert is sometimes easy to pick on, but today students give him their full respect, clapping and telling him they will miss him.

I took the floor. My legs felt weak. The words barely got past my tongue. "This has been my most difficult year here. You have taught me so much. I don't want to go, but I have no choice. We tried hard to make this as normal a school year as possible, fearing we would get closed down if we fought back too much. Maybe that wasn't right. I don't know. We did have a successful year in many ways and we have a great graduation planned." I had a hard time continuing. Manuel reentered the room. I gave him a hug as my tears began to fall. "I love you all and I'm going to miss you."

Elena moved to the center of the room as others began to cry and students came up to us for more hugs and handshakes. She said they would try their best to keep the school going, but no one is sure what is going to happen. "After graduation, we will be meeting again and trying to work something out with Adolfo. For the rest of today, let's try and enjoy ourselves and celebrate this year's graduating class."

We milled around for a few minutes as students and teachers began taking down tables and carrying them outside. Mothers retrieved their kids from the child care and stereo speakers were set up facing out to the boulevard. Cesar and Manuel hung a *piñata* from a rope tied to the oak tree in front of school and I tied the other end to the second-floor windowsill. Food, prepared by students' families, rolled out from the kitchen and half a dozen students' parents joined us as Alberto convened our last ceremony. Burning sage, he blessed the food and the graduates. Music filled the air. The party had begun.

GRADUATION IS ORGANIZED similar to our other activities. Graduates voted on where it would be held, what kind of food and music they wanted, and who would speak. They asked Sylvia to come back and be this year's commencement speaker.

Friday morning, as I signed in, the receptionist said Adolfo was looking for me. I dropped my belongings off in my office and went to see him. As I entered the door, he told me, "I'm canceling graduation. And I'm reprimanding all of the high school staff." What now? I asked him, "What are you talking about?" His response was to tell me, "There will be no graduation unless I am speaking and a board member speaks. I am canceling all requisitions for money and you will pay me back for any money already spent." I felt as though I was in a bad *Twilight Zone* episode. "And Sylvia is not allowed to speak at the graduation." "That is not possible," I answered. I explained to him the process we use and how the graduates themselves choose their speakers. "This is their day."

I felt mixed about Adolfo's threat to cancel the graduation. We could hold it somewhere else, but that would guarantee no staff would be returning next year. On the other hand, I could not make decisions for the students. I tried to reach a compromise with Adolfo. "I can take your suggestions back to the students," I proposed. "We will speak or there will be no graduation," he reiterated. "I can't cancel Sylvia," I said. "The students voted for her. They respect her and want her to be at their graduation." Adolfo never gives in on anything, but he seemed to grasp that it wouldn't be prudent to go against the students on this one. He told me they could have whomever they wanted as long as he and a board member were the first speakers. I told him I would meet with the students and see what we could work out.

I called the teachers and graduates together for a lunchtime meeting. I explained how Adolfo wanted to cut off funds and cancel the graduation unless we agreed to his terms. Students were the most vehement in denouncing Adolfo's demands. Manuel, to my surprise, and I argued for a compromise. I didn't feel good about it, but it seemed like our best option at the moment. The choice seemed to be to accept his terms or hold our own graduation at a new location and all get fired. I proposed that we tell Adolfo that he and a board member could speak first. After they sat down, we would continue with our graduation and try to forget about their being there. Reluctantly, students agreed.

GRADUATION WAS HELD in a second-floor theater room at a local church. Expansive, with a stage up front, it had only three small windows opening to an enclosed courtyard. We carted in four large fans, but nothing seemed to cut the heat and humidity. The decorations committee worked late into the night and the room was stunning with crepe paper draped along all the walls, flowers standing at the corners of the stage, and a long food table across the back covered with white tablecloths. At center stage stood a microphone stand ringed by chairs for the graduates. Rows of metal folding chairs lined the floor.

Students and their families began to fill the room. Dressed in suits and long dresses, graduates pulled their commencement gowns over their heads in the back room behind the stage. The only room in the building with air conditioning, it served as a sanctuary. As the DJ struck up the music, graduates filed out to the applause of the audience. Alexis introduced each student before asking Adolfo and the board president to speak. They were greeted with constrained clapping. Their words had the air of a funeral minister talking about a deceased he never knew.

The show must go on and on we went. Live music from a folkloric group, followed by Sylvia, followed by the presentation of diplomas, followed by food. It was too hot to waste time. We expedited everyone's remarks. As I stood in the empty room after clean-up, I became nostalgic for graduations past. Adolfo and Alfredo left before the food and the hugs, handshakes, and thank you's from student families. Even they could not ruin such a momentous event.

WE SETTLED INTO the last week of our contracts. As we talked together in the library, Stuart announced that he would not be returning. He will be looking for a job where he can work more closely with gay teens. That leaves only Alberto, Alexis, Angel, Cesar, and Elena as candidates. Looking at this group, Alberto proposed an all-Latino staff for September. "Now is the time," he said.

Alberto had pulled me aside before the meeting and asked me to speak in favor of his proposal to the full staff. "It is difficult for me to advise, counsel, or argue for anyone staying under the conditions set by Adolfo," I said. After the graduation fiasco, I have little confidence in him. At the same time, we had talked before about the possibility of an all-Latino staff. I gave a rundown of my first year here and the factionalism among the Latino staff and I retold the story of how I became the coordinator/principal. I suggested that the white and Latino staff who are not returning leave the room, letting the remaining staff see if they think they can become a viable group.

One outcome of their discussion was a proposal that we meet with Adolfo one more time to see if there is a basis for anyone staying on staff. Alberto went to speak with him. When he returned, he said, "He will meet with us this afternoon. He is angry, but I think we need to listen to what he is saying. This should be a time of healing. It can be different next year. I don't want any more backbiting from anyone. If I see it, I'll call you out right away. I am convinced we can work with Adolfo." Elena, Cesar, and I expressed our skepticism, but Alberto asked that we give the staff who may stay an opportunity to work it out.

ADOLFO WALKED INTO THE ROOM, sat down in a folding chair, faced the staff, and said, "I'm putting together a new philosophy for the high school. I will let you know what it is when I am done with it. Don't forget who signs the checks around here. And don't think you will be telling me who is returning in September. I will tell you who'll be back and who won't on Friday."

As a group, we were speechless. Adolfo continued. "You teachers are not doing your job. You unduly influence students so they don't think for themselves. This has to stop. I have my spies. They have told me what you're up to over here. I know about your secret meetings and how you use the computers and the copy machine." He pulled a piece of paper out of a folder he brought in with him. "See this? It is a copy of my directory. One of you is trying to get into my computer to see what I'm writing. You have never shown any respect for me. None of you ever say hello to me in the halls. I'm getting death threats on my phone and I blame you. I asked my cousin to come up here from San Antonio. He asked me where your families live because he is ready to go after them to get at the teachers who are harassing me."

It wasn't a happy meeting. The only teacher to speak was Alberto. "Things are workable for next year. There is a lot of anger on both sides, but we have to give it a try."

After Adolfo left the room, Alberto again spoke passionately about the possibility of an all-Latino staff and how he feels we can work with Adolfo. Cesar and Angel responded that after this last meeting, there is no way they can continue to teach here. "If it wasn't for Adolfo," Cesar told Alberto, "I would come back. The past weeks have made me physically ill. I can't work in this kind of environment." Elena and Alexis left the door open, saying they will continue to talk with Alberto.

I PULL MY CAR into the parking lot. It's Thursday morning. Two more days. The weather has cooled to the low 80s. I'm wearing shorts and a black T-shirt. I want to try to remain centered and not allow my anger or bitterness to cloud these last hours. I'm looking forward to the midsummer week Elena and I have planned with her newborn, my youngest daughter, and six of the young mothers and their children up at the camp where we held last year's retreat. It'll be our last outing together.

I greet the receptionist and check my box. I find a note from Loisa telling me she won't be able to go on the camping trip with her 2-year-old daughter. She was told by Carlotta that she would lose her part-time job here at Aztlan Alternative if she goes with Elena and me. Carlotta is the assistant to one of the members of the management team and Loisa's supervisor. So much for remaining calm.

I waited for Carlotta to show up in her office, letting everyone else I ran into know how upset I was. When I found out that she had arrived at work, I confronted her. She explained that Adolfo "ordered" her to tell Loisa she could not attend the camping trip. "You know what really bothers me?" I told her. "Adolfo is using Loisa to get back at me and the high school. I really don't care what they do to me anymore. This should be Loisa's decision whether to go and not Adolfo's. Now she is told it is a choice between losing her job and going on the camping trip with her child. This is unfair."

Carlotta looked at me with fear and anger in her eyes. "They'll get you for this if you continue to keep at it. Take my advice and just stay out of it." "What are they going to do," I said, "fire me?" She said they have ways to get me. "You need this reference." I was angry and lost all tact as Loisa walked in the room. "What reference? It'll be a cold day in hell when I'll ask these assholes for a reference. They're a bunch of crooked poverty pimps. If they want to get down and dirty, let's get down and dirty. I know where the skeletons are buried. Let's talk about the sexual harassment going on with some of the top administrators." I knew I had crossed a line I shouldn't be crossing, but I didn't care. I walked outside, where I saw Manuel.

I was in the middle of telling Manuel what had happened when Loisa came out. She said that Carlotta went straight to Adolfo and told him what I said. I knew I was in trouble now. As I walked back into the building, I passed Carlotta in the reception area. "Why did you go straight to Adolfo?" I asked her. "I had to," she said. "You said those things in front of Loisa. I beg you, Mark. Stay out of this. By the grace of God, leave it alone."

I went upstairs and found Alberto and Elena sitting in the library. I told them what just transpired. Alberto said he was about to go and meet with Adolfo and asked if I wanted him to bring this up. At first I hesitated. Then I told him it would be fine with me, but I don't want to go talk with him alone. "If he wants to talk and if you're willing to come in with me, then I'll do it. I don't want to battle him one on one. But, you don't have to argue my case, Alberto. I don't want to drag you into this." He left and returned 5 minutes later saying Adolfo would meet with the two of us.

I took a deep breath as we walked into Adolfo's office. I sat in the chair nearest the door. Alberto sat next to the window. Adolfo came out from behind his desk and started to sit in a folding chair near the wall. Halfway down, he stood back up. "You betrayed me. You're just a dirty white motherfucker. I have no respect for you." He turned to Alberto. "This just goes to prove you can't trust these white motherfuckers." Adolfo moved back toward me, pointing his finger at my face. I tried to remain calm. I said, "I would appreciate it if you would sit down."

I looked over to Alberto, who sat still. Adolfo moved within a foot of my chair. Leaning over me, face grimaced, he said, "We don't need white motherfuckers like you. I know where you live, you coward. You don't have the courage to go man to man with me." He moved his face within an inch of my mine, pointed his finger to his lip and demanded, "Go ahead, go ahead. Are you too coward?" I could feel and taste his anger. I didn't know if he was going to hit me, but I knew I needed to stay as motionless as possible. Seconds flashed by. I turned my head slightly toward Alberto and said, "This is what I mean." He looked to be in shock. Alberto finally blurted out, "Sit down, Adolfo." Stepping backward, Adolfo took his seat.

Adolfo pulled his chair up so we were about 6 feet apart. We both spoke at once. Adolfo accused me of wanting to go out with a big hurrah. "You planned all this," he told me. Referring to Carlotta, he said, "You will go to the women, but you're not man enough to come to me." I tried to explain why I was angry with him for ordering Loisa not to attend the camping trip. "You have no right to use her to try and get at me."

Alberto eventually succeeded in getting us to stop arguing and insisted that each of us be allowed to speak without the other one interrupting. He asked me to speak first. I reiterated what I had said about Loisa. "You crossed a line that really makes me angry. The issue for me is that you have no right to punish her as a way to get back at the high school or at me."

Adolfo responded that the "real point is you don't have the balls to come straight to me. Why did you have to go through someone else? In my eyes, you are the lowest of the low. I thought I had some respect for you, but not any more."

With Alberto in the room, I was feeling I should at least try to be diplomatic. I said I was wrong for "losing my cool" when talking with Carlotta. "But you have to understand how mad I am about this." I went on to explain that there are many things that get covered up in this agency and then people are ordered not to talk about them for fear of losing their jobs. "This is no secret. Deny it if you want, but you know it's true. You might not want to believe it, but people talk to each other. It's ironic to me that you accuse me of not coming to you, but at the same time you order staff not to talk to me."

Adolfo didn't answer directly. He sat back in his chair, looking at Alberto. "Carlotta was told Loisa had to make a choice. It is a special privilege to work here." I felt like saying, "What bullshit," but I restrained myself. "You're the responsible person, Adolfo. Somehow Loisa got the message she would be fired if she went with Elena and me. I believe that came from you."

Adolfo returned to his point that I "just wanted to go out with a last hurrah." I told him, "This is totally untrue. Actually, I think my practice over the past months has shown just the opposite. My personal goal these last days was to have a calm week, take care of business, and leave on my appointed day. You are the one who created this crisis, not me."

This got Adolfo out of his chair again. Alberto asked him to sit back down. Alberto wanted to speak. "I can see that both of you are hurt and angry, but we need to listen to each other and try and find some common ground. It is good you are now talking and this did not end in violence." He said a Native prayer and asked us to speak to each other again.

Adolfo faced Alberto. "I know I have to control my temper, but I have been hurt by Mark." He didn't apologize to me, but he said, "I am listening to him and I am sorry it got this far." For my part I reiterated my apology for talking out of line with Carlotta. "I am looking for one thing, a fair resolution so Loisa is given the opportunity to decide for herself whether she wants to go on the camping trip without undue pressure or under threat of being fired."

Alberto told Adolfo that my request was reasonable and he should consider it. Adolfo agreed. We all stood up. Adolfo and Alberto shook hands and hugged. Alberto and I hugged. Adolfo and I stood awkwardly facing each other. Alberto requested we shake hands. We did and I turned to leave. Adolfo asked Alberto to stay. He wanted to talk more.

I saw Alberto the next day outside my office. "I now believe what you have been telling me," he said. "You didn't believe me before?" I asked. He said he did but "it is different to experience it. I think yesterday's discussion went well and you came out on top." I said, "I feel like the most positive thing was there was a nonviolent resolution. I'm not sure there would have been if you hadn't been there." I packed up the last of my belongings and took my final walk out onto the boulevard.

36

Epilogue

Alberto, Elena, and Alexis decided to stay with the school. Adolfo agreed, but said final decisions would be made when they signed their new contracts on September first. At noon on her first day back, Elena was called in for a meeting. She was told that there was a discrepancy in her funder paperwork. She was fired on the spot. Alexis was called in next and told they also found discrepancies in her paperwork. She was issued a warning, but given the opportunity to stay. She resigned. Five months later she gave birth to a baby boy. Alberto remained with the new staff. He sharply criticized the previous teachers for our inability to control students, giving them too much freedom.

The corporatization of the agency was completed with Adolfo and Alfredo instituting a profit-sharing plan. Although seemingly unethical in a not-for-profit, employee salaries were now based on numbers of clients served. Less than half of the previous high school students returned. One student, after being arrested, was told he was no longer welcome in the school because he gave it a "bad image." Another student, a gang leader and outspoken in his criticisms of the administration, attended school regularly during the fall session. Needing a full year's credits to graduate, he was met at the door when he attempted to return in January, handed his diploma, and told he was no longer allowed in the school since he was a graduate.

Cesar took a position as an organizer with another community not-for-profit. Manuel moved out of state and now works as a counselor in a public school in a Mexican community. Robert moved to a small town, hired on as a youth counselor, and works part-time as a disc jockey. Angel works for a Spanish-language media firm doing educational videos. Sylvia is the director of a youth empowerment program. Elena is director of a university bilingual development program for public school teachers. She also initiated a GED preparation project with former Aztlan Alternative students.

Eloisa is working full-time as a retail clerk; Martha gave birth and is enrolled in a business college; Lena and Tony are studying for their GED; and Javier was arrested and sentenced to 6 months for weapons possession.

In the summer following graduation, five mothers and their children joined Elena and me and our young daughters for a family camping trip at the cooperative summer camp. We mourned the death of the high school, but hopes were still high with the thought that Elena would be returning to the school. Four of the five mothers have since left school. One expressed interest in Elena's GED project. Loisa did not go on the trip. She earned a college scholarship and elected to go to a local private university. Her plans are currently on hold as she is at home after giving birth to her second child.

PART III

THE ROAD TRAVELED: CREATING AN ENGAGED PEDAGOGY

Looking beyond the immediate. Stretching the boundaries of acceptability. Documenting life experiences as they happen. Being subjective. Asking unasked questions. Naming the unnameable. Throughout this journey, the characteristic or issue that often rose to the surface was race. While not appearing in every story, it lay in wait, ready to rear its head, project itself into the debate, sway an argument, highlight contradictions. Race became more than color, more than ethnicity or culture, determining so much and alone determining only surface realities. Impacted by gender, economics, class, sexual orientation, and cultural subcontexts, race became an essential and complex signifier of record.

What does it mean when a teacher is one of the only (if not *the* only) white faces in the classroom? Who are we, white educators who choose to teach students of color and work collaboratively with teachers of color? What is our role? Can we be effective? How are our responsibilities different because of race, ethnicity, and privilege? My initial thoughts were that I would be examining white teachers, our projections of race, our teaching practices vis-à-vis students of color, and our working relationships with teachers of color. While this is still the heart of this inquiry, the map widened quickly when I realized that race alone, while a predominating factor, lives in a multifaceted world of identities, subidentities, and power relationships. To predominate whiteness as the sole frame of reference would limit and essentially invalidate the entire work, although the dilemma remained—white was still *my* seeing eye.

Racism is an endemic component of life in our society. Short of radical restructuring, there will be no early end to the vast discrepancies that exist between whites and people of color in terms of substantive issues such as poverty, infant mortality, imprisonment rates, and the more subjective but no less violent daily institutionalized injustices and inequities. Is it possible to find cracks, to work in the margins where questions can be asked—and answered? Places where alternatives can be dreamed and developed? Where race transcends to higher levels? Toni Morrison (1992) writes that "the world does not become raceless or will not become unracialized by assertion" (p. 46), but is it possible to create a reconceptualization, or revisualization, where race becomes a holistic force for change within a broad framework of social issues?

In my mind I picture an Alcoholics Anonymous–type meeting. We sit around in a circle, speaking in soft tones. A cup of coffee in my hand, I inform the group: My name is Mark and I am a racist. Actually, I once attended an unlearning-racism workshop that looked like an AA gathering and I brought up this analogy. I was given quite the nasty look by the white facilitator. Undaunted, I find that the question becomes how to translate this recognition and yearning to be different, to chart a path in form and content that leads to a changing and transformed practice through actual participation in situations where a transformed practice is necessitated and desired.

Wait a minute. What kind of participation are we talking about here? There is a line, sometimes thin, more often blatant, although seldom recognized by the white practitioners, between genuine transformation and antiracist appropriations (Crenshaw, 1992). Who ultimately has power and authority? I was constantly perplexed by my position at Aztlan Alternative High School as the supervisor-designate for the staff and authority figure to many students and their parents. Is it possible to be un-authority or anti-authority and still maintain a position of authority? When Sal told me he could never work "under" a white person, but was willing to give it a try, I felt set up. But I did it anyway.

A year after leaving Aztlan Alternative, I accepted a position in a self-defined progressive teacher education program in another city. Although the faculty and administrators were nearly all white, I was encouraged by a philosophy that spoke of teachers as change agents, stressed multiculturalism, and listed democratic education as its ideal and practice. The program attracted adults who yearned to ask questions, challenge the status quo, and teach in new ways. Behind this picture of social activism and democracy I found hierarchies, stressed-out students, silenced faculty, and a program driven by state education mandates. I started asking questions. Why is lesson planning seen and taught as the focus and essence of curriculum and instruction? Shouldn't we be helping students ask what is worthwhile to know and experience? In staff meetings, why was I so often feeling as though I were in a bad B-movie sitting in the teachers' lounge from hell listening to students and faculty being denigrated? Speaking out only brought retributions and reprisals. The act of asking questions about worth and knowledge led to my being summoned to a one-on-one meeting with the program director, who stated that she was "shocked" by my queries. Needless to say, my contract was not renewed and once again I was pushed out of a teaching position.

While still employed, I had the opportunity to work with a group of teachers in the local public schools who teach students expelled from their regular schools or who are on probation, living in group homes, or in juvenile detention. At a professional development workshop, I gave a presentation on using writing as a method to motivate students and increase basic skills and critical and creative thinking. I began by trying to set some context, which led to using 2 of our allotted 3 hours talking about the implications of working with this population of students and our roles and responsibilities as teachers. Looking around the room, I noticed that about 80% of the 35 teachers were white. As I traveled around to their schools, it was just as evident that the percentage of students of color was higher than the 60% they represented in the district.

I unexpectedly caused a furor in the workshop by questioning our roles in these types of reentry programs and alternative schools. A noticeable tension surfaced in the room as I presented documentation showing that transitional, reentry, or last-chance alternatives exhibit little or no long-term correlation of success between what goes on in the programs and the level of dropouts, suspensions, and expulsions (Raywid, 1995). I stated that this was not necessarily a case of us, as teachers, not being highly motivated or experienced, but that what works in our programs is not replicated in regular public schools. The stated purpose of these reentry and transitional programs is to prepare students to successfully reenter schools that failed them initially.

One teacher asked: "What's the point in continuing to teach if what I do doesn't work?" His negative tone in asking the question made me want to say, maybe you *shouldn't* be teaching here, but better judgment prevailed. I used an analogy. Save someone from drowning, teach them to be expert mechanics or great chefs, then throw them back into the water. Will they be able to survive? What are we doing in these so-called alternative programs when our students are not succeeding back in their original schools? Are we functioning as safety or escape valves for a public school system that does not want to acknowledge or take responsibility for the students who do not succeed in its schools? Toward the end of our discussion, the program director added that in a recent survey of 100 of their students, only 8 successfully made the transition back to school.

My original intent in asking the question about the purpose and intent of the schools in which we work was to create a framework for introducing the use of writing with "at-risk" and marginalized students. I didn't realize how much questions of worth and personal self-justification would surface as the main issues. Coincidence or not, in this setting it was only the white teachers who questioned the appropriateness and consequences of the question.

EVEN THOUGH I lost that last teaching position for asking what is worthwhile to know and experience, the question of worth, knowledge, and experience still guides my work (Schubert, 1986). In looking at the philosophy and pedagogy that propelled my work as a teacher and principal at two urban alternative high schools for "dropouts" from the 1980s into the late 1990s, I was never able to come up with a satisfactory answer when people asked me if and how both schools could be replicated. There were many reasons for our success—small schools, small classes, relevant curriculum, democratic processes, and student involvement. I knew there was more to be said, but I always felt hesitant answering the question because every situation is different. At the same time, I wanted to better understand how and what we did so I could articulate it to others, especially urban white teachers who seek to be antiracist.

I was also resistant to writing down anything that looked like an educational paradigm. Charting this kind of blueprint goes against my nature. These types of frameworks imply (at least to me) certainty, conformity, predictability, and standardization. My search was much more for ambiguity, complexity, and nuance. I was more interested in description of experiences and processes than in outcomes. At the same time, the outcomes were overwhelmingly positive at each school. They just weren't easily measured, at least not by the usual standards of assessment. In the current climate of standardization, testing, and increased teacher accountability, this is a hard concept to sell. Yet, when we challenge the concept that accountability need not be synonymous with test scores, we also have to create valid and credible alternative modes of assessing students' and teachers' growth and performance.

In trying to broach the tension between measurement standards and narrative description, I finally pieced together a framework based on the belief that teaching is an art and not primarily a technical task. Not discounting the importance of technique, training, and expertise, I sought to see the driving force of teaching as engagement of both students and teachers (Haberman, 1996). Reflecting on my own teaching, talking with other practitioners, visiting teachers at schools with similar populations, and researching relevant literature pushed me to create a succinct description of a holistic framework that explained the pedagogical life of Aztlan Alternative High School. I call it an *engaged pedagogy*. It encompasses four main components: *cultural relevancy, teacher reflection,* a *pedagogy of hope,* and *teachers as researchers.* Listed below are the subcomponents within each area:

Cultural Relevancy

- Academics
- Culture
- Critical Thinking

Teacher Reflection

- Experience + Reflection = Growth
- Autobiography

Pedagogy of Hope

- Risk Taking
- Insinuating Complexity

Teachers as Researchers

- Valuing Teacher Voices
- Collaboration

The entire *engaged pedagogy* framework is rooted in three underpinnings or pillars:

- social construction of meaning
- student-centeredness
- democracy and dialogue

Together, the above components, subcomponents, and pillars serve as a theoretical portrait developed over a decade of collaborative work in alternative high school settings. My hope is that this engaged pedagogy framework can serve as a guide or jumping-off point for others who want to teach in or create similar types of schools. For white educators in particular, my desire is that it can serve as a frame of reference for those of us who strive to be antiracist and progressive in our teaching and a way to look at our own work, ask questions, name and understand what is working and what is not, and recontextualize and reshape our work as white teachers.

Within the framework, the cultural relevancy component is based on two assumptions: (1) the need for antiracist education and pedagogy committed to social justice and issues of diversity, equity, and democracy; and (2) the moving of the question, *do* race, gender, and class impact on education and teaching to *how* do race, gender, and class impact. This movement allows for the possibility of looking at the implications of these social constructs and the creation of an alternative practice based not solely on critique but on a supportive environment where mistakes are seen as an implicit part of the process and not something that calls the whole into question. As William Pinar writes:

> Anti-racist education resides at the heart of education, as it requires commitments to justice, freedom, and diversity to be enacted in the context of daily institutional life, rather than murmured as a litany for a world yet to come. (Pinar, Reynolds, Slattery, and Taubman, 1995, p. 357)

One of our goals in implementing cultural relevancy was to try to move beyond and transform a standard definition of multiculturalism (McCarthy, 1993). In doing this, we sought to recognize overt issues of power, privilege, and authority, which necessitated talking honestly about concurrent social issues such as white supremacy, patriarchy, racism, sexism, and homophobia. We also sought *not* to essentialize identities or separate cultures and ethnicities into holidays, months, or foods, thus striving for a more holistic (and political) approach. Instead of viewing holidays as add-ons to the curriculum, events such as Cinco de Mayo and Día de los Muertos were looked at as spiritual and political as well as cultural celebrations. They became personal and collective days of reflection and action, such as setting up a community altar and arts exhibition. By integrating open discussion of oppression into the full curriculum, we attempted to balance oppression and resistance into a liberatory pedagogy (Freire, 1970, 1985). Implementation was guided by Gloria Ladson-Billings' (1995) theory of culturally relevant pedagogy, which posits three criteria for evaluating success: "an ability to develop students academically, a willingness to nurture and support cultural competence, and the development of a sociopolitical or critical consciousness" (p. 483).

The essence of our approach to academics can be summed up as striving for intellectual engagement and high academic expectations and performance, and looking at new and flexible ways of teaching. In raising expectations, it redefined academic excellence for all students, seeing competence and excellence as a socially as well as academically defined standard that takes into account diversity and individual differences. We were also confronted with an exorbitant number of students who had been classified as special education and who had, in turn, internalized this designation to the point of believing that they were not as smart or talented as others. One of our responses to the classification of students and the subsequent dumbing down of the curriculum (Gatto, 1992) that consistently occurs in traditional schools was to refuse to accept school records when students entered Aztlan Alternative High School. Financially, we paid a price because we could have received state monies for all students who voluntarily signed themselves in as special education designees. We also did not ask students about their special education status unless they volunteered it. One positive consequence of this decision was seeing students make phenomenal academic advances and together marveling at how they had previously been placed in the "dummy" classes at their other schools.

With all "good" intentions, I once set up a reading class for students who were well below grade level, students who had been in my regular reading/literature classes but who I thought could benefit from a more collective and supportive environment. The first two classes had the feeling of a morgue. I finally asked the students what was happening. They informed me that, looking around the room, they saw the same grouping of students who had been together since grade school, always in the dummy class for the slow readers. I apologized for not talking with them ahead of time and offered to place them back in regular classes. After more discussion, they decided to keep this format because we at least had the issue out in the open. I can honestly report that it was one of the most fulfilling classes I have ever taught.

Our decision to use a cultural-relevancy approach to academics meant that we encouraged the use of multiple approaches and styles for teaching and assessment, including cooperative learning, team-teaching, multilevel classrooms, project-based and hands-on learning, and finding new and relevant source materials. This included the use of first-person narratives; the creation of our own materials, such as new canons of relevant literature; and the introduction of innovative, integrated, content-specific, and cross-subject curricula. Not every experiment worked. At one point, we mandated team-teaching for every class. It was a disaster. We learned that this dogmatic use of a good idea soon turned into its opposite. For some pairs of teachers it created new possibilities and led to better teaching. For other pairs, it only brought out each individual's worst attributes. It took students to demand that we end the experiment because they had to be in the classroom with the dysfunctional pairings. Fortunately, we responded quickly and changed teaching assignments before the midpoint of the quarter.

We instituted multilevel classes in all subject areas in an attempt to end tracking and ability grouping of students. I abandoned the "slow readers" class the following quarter and we later made two other adjustments. In the math classes, we reconstituted subject-level ability grouping with the option of students' moving at their own pace without having to rely on changing classes at the designated quarter breaks. In the sciences, we created a required class for all new students that served as an introduction to our project-based and community-centered philosophy and methodology in teaching the sciences and as a place to create a minimum standard in science proficiency for all students to advance to subject-based science classes.

Utilizing a culturally relevant context created an additional challenge for the white teachers to rethink a nonracist or color-blind approach (Ladson-Billings, 1994) that obliterates difference. This, in turn, allowed the white teachers to acknowledge and take responsibility for being part of the dominant culture while simultaneously being part of creating new and alternative practices and ways of being. Not that this struggle was smooth. For all their faith-based intentions, the present and former religious volunteers who stayed on as teachers seldom seemed to fully comprehend the contradictory nature of their relationships to students and the community in which the school was located. Robert's insistence on using Christian rock and other music he deemed relevant even over the objection of his students was left unresolved. I recently read a book by another white teacher, Mark Gerson (1996), that graphically highlights the pitfalls of this racial blind spot. Gerson presents himself as an empathetic white who grew up in a wealthy suburb of New Jersey, graduated from an elite private university, was accepted into Yale Law School, and decided to defer entrance while teaching in an "inner-city" school. The narrative of this self-described neoconservative reads as if he "slummed" for a year with the poor. A prime example of how not to be as a white person teaching students of color, he constantly imposed his cultural values in the classroom. Never questioning his stratified and tracked classes of

Black and Latino students, Gerson exhibited a know-it-all attitude that smacked of white privilege and patronization as he openly challenged multicultural education, one example being his insistence that his students speak "the Queen's English" to the exclusion of all other language forms in class.

The culture subcomponent of cultural relevancy works to use students' prior knowledge and experiences as a basis to explore their own and other peoples' cultures with a strong emphasis on language. Ideologically, this came to a curricular head when Dr. Williams came to discuss Afrocentrism with the staff and during our internal debates pitting Mexican against Chicano nationalism. These discussions also became problematic for the white teachers because there was always an undercurrent from some of the Latino staff of feeling uncomfortable having these discussions with silent whites in the room. I faced the additional lose-lose dilemma of having opinions, stating them, and then being criticized not for the content of my thoughts, but for the fact that I presented them in the first place. When it became clear that Manuel, Alexis, Cesar, and Andrea were more upset with my writing on the subject of Mexican-centrism and bringing Dr. Williams than with the content of her presentation, we were caught between the proverbial rock and a hard place. The same contradiction arose around supervision of staff. Ironically, when Sylvia took over day-to-day supervision, complaints continued but without the underpinning of my perceived racism.

Acquiring the tools of critical thinking was crucial to implementing our curriculum. For us, the heart of critical thinking was learning how to think and then applying that knowledge in academic and practical settings. At its best, it was the teaching of how to think as opposed to what to think. This did not mean that teachers wouldn't express their opinions, but that our views and students' views would be constantly open to interrogation, reflection, debate, and introspection. Projects, content units, and learning experiences ranged from personal and school issues to student- and community-identified problems, such as the need for and subsequent creation of the on-site child-care center for student mothers.

Embodied in the concept of teacher reflection is the notion of teaching as an ongoing process of learning, exemplified in the equation experience + reflection = growth (Posner, 1996). To be effective, engaged, and antiracist teachers, we must look at what and how we teach. As we construct meaning through our experiences, this reflection on our teaching and learning propels the growth process individually and collectively. Without this perspective, our work can too easily become bogged down in the techniques of teaching without our being aware that this is happening. We then lose our ability to ask the crucial questions that move a curriculum forward, a process Posner (1995) names "reflective eclecticism." In other words, having the tools to ask what is worthwhile to know and experience based on our own experiences and acquiring an experiential continuum (Dewey, 1938) from which to further reflect and grow, are our best safeguards against personal and pedagogical stagnation.

As a self-defined collaborative, the staff at Aztlan Alternative High School constantly worked to build in time for discussion. Excessively long meetings and frustration at not being able to make quick decisions sometimes characterized our attempts, but we also built a bond among ourselves that allowed a level of trust that is not often present in school faculties. It also meant taking risks, such as allowing our teaching to be evaluated by an independent student committee and being open to different modes of interrelating—for example, participating in the sweat toward the end of our tenure at Aztlan Alternative High School. Even though the sweat marked the culmination of a process, our ability to function as a group and to unite with others, such as during the strike or as we constantly reworked the curriculum, was rooted in the need to name and talk through issues that we thought could build a stronger and more viable school for the students and the community.

A positive consequence of this approach was the mirroring of our efforts among the students. Two prime examples were the student evaluation committee and the actions of the group of returning students who intervened during the period when we were integrating new staff into the school. In each instance, student initiative created and led the actions taken by the students with the teachers. Reflection was also incorporated into our assessment procedures with students through biquarterly written self-evaluations and conferences.

One problematic with this approach was the degree to which individual teachers were able to internalize self-reflection. I generally thought that group discussions and working directly with students absorbed so much of our time and energy that other areas, such as personal reflection, were slighted and lacked institutional support. It is in this arena that I believe autobiography plays an essential role as a cornerstone to the effectiveness of self-reflection and a means to identify significant and transformative learning experiences in our own lives. By naming for ourselves and others those moments that stand out as powerful learning experiences and by looking at the nature of those experiences and the conditions that brought them about, we can begin to incorporate some of these processes into our teaching, the goal being to help our students become, themselves, self-reflective and engaged in their learning and their lives. To teach it we have to do it (Fried, 1995; Graham, 1991; Kohl, 1994).

For white teachers working in a school and community where most of the few other whites are in real or symbolically authoritative positions (such as police officers, medical professionals, or case workers and social workers), it becomes imperative that we challenge our concepts of self and community. Our choices must include personal accountability (Ayers, 1989) if we are to lay the basis for a transformed practice that acknowledges difference, combats a color-blind approach (Ladson-Billings, 1994), yet also reaffirms a positive self-identity (Howard, 1999). Who we are in relation to the schools and communities in which we work may be initially predetermined by skin color and the dominant white society's preconceptions of the community's cultural norms, but this is an ongoing conundrum that we must consistently address in a positive acknowledgment of difference.

For white teachers to effectively challenge both our own and societal preconceptions based on dominant political or cultural norms that often initially shape white peoples' relationships with people of color, we need to look for alternative frameworks in which to think about and conceptualize our roles as teachers. Personally, I have found the concept of *currere* to be invaluable. Defined as a "structure of meaning that follows from past situations, but which contains, perhaps unarticulated, contradictions of past and present as well as images of possible futures" (Pinar et. al., 1995, p. 520), *currere* is a "call to examine one's response to a text, response to an idea, response to a colleague, in ways which invite depth, understanding, and transformation of that response" (Pinar, 1994, 119). Pinar further describes the process as follows:

> Pragmatic action cannot be frozen into principles and concepts . . . and to the extent one enters this arena with static principles of how to behave, one deforms the situation. Necessarily one has shaped, let us say, the pedagogic situation and selected out many possibilities. . . . One is, if rigid or mindless of the importance of offering oneself up to social experience, automatically freezing the Other into his or her position as well. (p. 118)

Ironically, both of these phenomena—dogmatic concepts and immersion in the social experience—were in operation at Aztlan Alternative High School. At varying times, the white and Latino teachers both fell back on preconceived notions of each other (Otherness), framed by their relationships to the dominant society and their personal experiences. In carrying out "debates over legitimate representation and over who has or ought to have the power to represent" (Pagano, 1990, p. 134), we created a collaborative and cooperative approach that eventually led to naming and resolving many of our conflicts. Often tense and filled with spoken and silent animosities, we gave new meaning to the adage "been down so long it looks like up to me." Perseverance and an articulated commitment to the process of collaboration and putting many of our racial complexities out on the table for discussion helped create a lively and alternative mode of staff interaction.

Lastly, self-reflection and autobiography offer a vehicle through which to interrogate whiteness (hooks, 1990) from an antiracist perspective that allows both acknowledgment of privilege and the necessity of and belief in self-transformation. Applying *currere* to this type of interrogation, Edgerton (1996) builds on the initial theories by offering a *currere* of marginality that looks at the "location" of whites in the center and people of color in the margins of dominant white society. She explains:

> The ways in which marginalized groups, individuals, and ideas come to be marginalized in a given culture, society, and/or place has much to do with what is considered to be knowledge and who is considered to possess it— who is perceived as knower and who is perceived as known. Clearly, education is deeply implicated in these processes. . . . The margin must "know" the center in order to survive, but the reverse is not true to the same extent. Yet neither margin nor center exists as such without the other. Hence, there is an infusion of each in the other. (pp. 37–38)

What this offers to white teachers is the opportunity to honestly place ourselves within the dominant society while at the same time positioning ourselves in marginal or alternative environments without, it is hoped, self-righteously believing that we "know all" about the students we teach and the colleagues of color with whom we work and collaborate. As teachers we become students and, in turn, internalize and integrate into our teaching an antiracist pedagogy and practice.

A pedagogy of hope rests on two tenets: (1) a belief in the essential goodness in people and the corollary that all students can succeed and (2) the idea that what we see in someone is what we are looking for. As Herbert Kohl (1994) writes:

> If you look at a child through the filter of her or his environment or economic status, and make judgments through the filters of your own cultural, gender, and racial biases, you'll find the characteristics you expect.

You'll also find yourself well placed to reproduce failure and to develop resistance in some children, a false sense of superiority in others. On the other hand, if you look for strengths and filter the world through the prism of hope, you will see and encourage the unexpected flowering of child life in the most unlikely places. (p. 44)

At Aztlan Alternative High School this translated into a teaching practice that looked for what was right, not what was wrong, in students and in their work. It openly challenged a deficit model of viewing students and their needs. It stressed the positive and aimed to use strengths to overcome weaknesses. It also offered the moral and social challenge to teachers to look at every child in our classrooms as if she or he were our own. In working with new teachers, I ask them to think, when they make decisions regarding individual students, if they would make the same choices if this student were their own child. If not, why not?

Incorporating a pedagogy of hope into our curriculum did not guarantee student success, but it often became the difference in changing a student's outlook and self-perception. When Angela stood up to Oscar when he attempted to close the on-site child-care center, she rose up for herself, her daughter, her community, and the whole of the student body, exhibiting a newfound leadership that served as a catalyst for other students as well. Taking responsibility for her own learning took on new dimensions for Angela far beyond grades or credit for course work.

It was a regrettable truism that we also seldom had students enter our doors who believed they would ever go to college. Many were the first in their families to graduate from high school. As our students began to win scholarships and enter local community colleges and state universities, newer students started to talk about going to college too. Unfortunately, we also discovered that many of our graduates were having a difficult time transitioning into postsecondary education without the support base they were used to at the high school. We would see graduates return to use the computers and talk to teachers, but our resources were much too limited to offer more than cursory help and assistance.

One consequence of a pedagogy of hope was the opening of doors to greater risk-taking and a view that risk-taking was at the center of good teaching. For us, this meant asking questions. It became our way of knowing and being in the world. It saw making mistakes as a natural part of the learning process, the key becoming our ability and willingness to identify and learn from our mistakes. Risk-taking, "action and reflection on the world in order to change it" (hooks, 1994, p. 14), and an engaged pedagogy pushed the proverbial envelope as we sought to constantly evolve as a school. We looked to change our teaching and the structures of the school whenever necessary to move forward. In social studies, science, the arts, math, English language arts—and in our decision to teach Spanish as a language arts and not as a foreign language—we sought to develop an interdisciplinary approach that combined antiracist and racial and ethnic positive theories and practice with a democratic process.

The issue of language is a good example of our evolution. Breaking with the Spanish I, II, III structure, we created Spanish language arts classes on an academic par with the English-language classes. We also set up bilingual classes in which students could work in their self-chosen language(s), including co-usage of Spanish and English, working to create a safe environment where we could "acknowledge and validate students' home language without using it to limit students' potential" (Delpit, 1993, 293). It should also be noted that we took an approach somewhat different from the one Delpit advocates. Seeking cultural and language fluency in both Spanish and English, Elena Hernández and I co-taught bilingual writing and separately taught Spanish and English language arts classes. One of our goals was to go beyond Spanish-language maintenance to higher levels of fluency and literacy. We advocated the use of English as an "emancipatory tool" (p. 294), but we did not tell students that they are the "inheritors and rightful heirs" (p. 294) of this dominant cultural discourse. We created instead a dual language approach that tried to take the best of both worlds to challenge the dominant English discourse while learning to use and manipulate it (Gamboa & Hernández, 1995).

Insinuating complexity (Kohl, 1994) is viewing knowledge critically and seeing issues and problems as relative and relational. This does not mean that there are no rights and wrongs; it does look at values and morals. What it strived to accomplish in our curriculum was to problematize, to look for the proverbial gray areas, to go below the surface and beyond accepted definitions and judgments. It deconstructed, but did so to create the ability to reconstruct, take action, and create alternatives. When we were successful, as with the all-school strike, the infusion of culture and the arts, and the revamping of the science and language programs, the school grew qualitatively. When our alternatives were met with institutional resistance that we could not combat, such as the reign of Adolfo, it meant the demise of the school.

Aztlan Alternative High School was openly and unabashedly

student-centered, yet the key to our ability to create a school that worked for and with students rested first and foremost with the teachers. This may sound contradictory, but we discovered, as did Marantz Cohen (1991) in her study of veteran teachers, that self-actualization among teachers benefits students. At Aztlan Alternative High School we took it a step further. Breaking with the individualization and compartmentalization inherent in traditional teaching, we sought a more dialectic relationship, a spiral development in which individual and collective growth reinforced each other. We openly asked the question: Who creates or should create curriculum? In doing so, we acknowledged and valued teachers' voices. We redefined the concept of teachers as researchers, creating a space that allowed us to tell our stories and give voice to our experiences and expectations. We openly sought, as Robert Fried (1995) promotes, to change the *game* of school. Breaking with the traditional and institutionalized top-down research-and-development curriculum design model, we created an alternative, collaborative process among all parties—teachers, students, school staff, the broader school community, and teacher education. Not only was this more equitable, but its range of involvement included many who would normally be disenfranchised or left out of the loop, including parents and community members. At its heart, our process was participatory, collaborative, and inclusive of students; most particularly, it placed a high degree of responsibility and accountability on our teachers, much more so than in regular schools.

Every house is built on a foundation and the underpinnings or pillars of this conceptual framework are (1) the social construction of meaning, (2) student-centeredness, and (3) dialogue, discussion, and democracy.

The social construction of meaning asks this question: How is meaning constructed? Contrary to the view that meaning is handed down by others or the research-and-development approach noted above, it says that knowing is a multidimensional social construction. We have and create experiences. "Each of our students brings a unique disposition into the classroom [and] each teacher carries a unique disposition with her or him" (Kincheloe, 1993, p. 108). Most importantly, this form of critical constructivism (Kincheloe, 1993) allows learning to come from naming and solving problems and issues. As Elliot Eisner (1991) writes:

> Human knowledge is a constructed form of experience and therefore a reflection of mind as well as nature: Knowledge is made, not simply discovered. (p. 7)

Student-centeredness, as described throughout this narrative and text, seeks to value and validate students' prior knowledge and prior experience. Starting with student concerns and lived experiences, it jointly and collaboratively creates projects and curriculum that combine student experience with content, or what is called the knowledge of the disciplines. As teachers, we try to concretize the process and make it real, helping students obtain the tools and information to be able to take responsibility for their own learning.

Dialogue, discussion, and democracy are, in many ways, the glue that holds this entire framework together. One of our goals was the creation of a democratic environment throughout the school and the curriculum beginning with the teaching staff and including the whole of the student body. Connected to and incumbent on a student-centered, democratic pedagogy is the necessity *not* to shy away from social issues or difficult questions. Ironically, while many schools defer these questions or limit their discussion, in this kind of democratic community of learners, such discussion works to engender student self-confidence and expression and student-teacher trust. In these types of learning situations, students are allowed and encouraged to examine the relationship between self and society as individuals and within the various communities in which they live. One of the positive consequences is that when students look at their own actions, negative behaviors within a school setting make less sense because of their vested interest in the process and outcomes. Alternative ways of being and learning are created and of value to students as they truly begin to take responsibility for their own learning. Even at the retreat, this commitment to democracy and discussion helped build a stronger and more viable learning community within the school.

In the end, this engaged pedagogy framework is just that—a framework, a theoretical portrait grounded in over 10 years of work in alternative school settings. It is an integral component of a holistic view of teaching and learning that looks at the teacher, learner, subject matter, and learning environment from multiple and interlinking perspectives. Can this framework be of use to others? Can it serve as a catalyst for more discussion and future change?

My passions for alternative education are hopefully evident within these writings, yet I am struck by the overuse and simplification currently attached to the word alternative. When I use the word in conversations, I get bemused looks. When pushed to explain, administrators, teachers, parents, and even students associate alternative with "troubled" students, students with behavioral issues, or boot camp style schools, institutions a teacher friend calls penal schools. Alternative has too often come to mean remedial education based in rigid direct instruction models, warehousing of students no other schools want, or post-hippie free schools with no rules or accountability. Maybe the role of alternatives is to be the forebearers of change. I would hope that we could utilize the successes and innovations of alternative education to push other schools to take risks, believe in their teachers and students, and become models for school reform. It is with this thought that I leave you to take what is useful in this book into your schools and to continually ponder what is worthwhile to know and experience.

References

Acuña, R. (1981). *Occupied America: A history of Chicanos.* New York: Harper and Row.

Ayers, W. (1989). *The good preschool teacher.* New York: Teachers College Press.

Crenshaw, K. (1992). Whose story is it, anyway? Feminist and antiracist appropriations of Anita Hill. In T. Morrison (Ed.), *Race-ing, justice, engendering power: Essays on Anita Hill, Clarence Thomas, and the construction of social reality* (pp. 402–440). New York: Pantheon.

Delpit, L. (1993). The politics of teaching literate discourse. In T. Perry & J. W. Fraser (Eds.), *Freedom's plow: Teaching in a multicultural classroom* (pp. 285–295). New York: Routledge.

Dewey, J. (1938). *Experience and education.* New York: Collier.

Edgerton, S. E. (1996). *Translating the curriculum: Multiculturalism into cultural studies.* New York: Routledge.

Eisner, E. W. (1991). *The enlightened eye: Qualitative inquiry and the enhancement of educational practice.* New York: Macmillan.

Freire, P. (1970). *Pedagogy of the oppressed.* New York: Continuum.

Freire, P. (1985). *The politics of education: Culture, power, and liberation.* South Hadley, MA: Bergin and Garvey.

Fried, R. L. (1995). *The passionate teacher: A practical guide.* Boston: Beacon.

Gamboa, G., & Hernández, J. (1995). Whole Spanish, Español: Observations at an alternative high school. Unpublished manuscript.

Gatto, J. T. (1992). *Dumbing us down: The hidden curriculum of compulsory schooling.* Philadelphia: New Society.

Gerson, M. (1996). *In the classroom.* New York: Macmillan

Graham, R. J. (1991). *Reading and writing the self: Autobiography in education and the curriculum.* New York: Teachers College Press.

Haberman, M. (1996). The pedagogy of poverty versus good teaching. In W. Ayers & P. Ford (Eds.), *City kids, city teachers: Reports from the front row* (pp. 118–130). New York: The New Press.

hooks, b. (1990). *Yearning: Race, gender, and cultural politics.* Boston: South End.

hooks, b. (1994). *Teaching to transgress: Education as the practice of freedom.* New York: Routledge.

Howard, G. R. (1999). *We can't teach what we don't know: White teachers, multiracial schools.* New York: Teachers College Press.

Kincheloe, J. L. (1993). *Toward a critical politics of teacher thinking: Mapping the postmodern.* Westport, CT: Bergin and Garvey.

Kohl, H. (1994). *"I won't learn from you" and other thoughts on creative maladjustment.* New York: The New Press.

Ladson-Billings, G. (1994). *The dreamkeepers: Successful teachers of African American children.* San Francisco: Jossey-Bass.

Ladson-Billings, G. (1995). Toward a theory of culturally relevant pedagogy. *American Educational Research Journal, 32*(3), 465–491.

Marantz Cohen, R. (1991). *A lifetime of teaching: Portraits of five veteran high school teachers.* New York: Teachers College Press.

McCarthy, C. (1993). After the canon: Knowledge and ideological representation in the multicultural discourse on curriculum reform. In C. McCarthy & W. Crichlow (Eds.), *Race, identity, and representation in education* (pp. 289–305). New York: Routledge.

Morrison, T. (1992). *Playing in the dark: Whiteness and the literary imagination.* Cambridge, MA: Harvard University Press.

Pagano, J. A. (1990). *Exiles and communities: Teaching in the patriarchal wilderness.* Albany, NY: SUNY Press.

Pinar, W. F. (1994). *Autobiography, politics, and sexuality: Essays in curriculum theory, 1972–1992, Vol. 2.* New York: Peter Lang.

Pinar, W. F., Reynolds, W. M., Slattery, P., & Taubman, P. M. (Eds.). (1995). *Understanding curriculum: An introduction to the study of historical and contemporary curriculum discourses.* New York: Peter Lang.

Posner, G. (1995). *Analyzing the curriculum* (2nd ed.). New York: McGraw-Hill.

Posner, G. (1996). *Field experience: A guide to reflective teaching* (4th ed.). White Plains, NY: Longman.

Raywid, R. A. (1995). Alternatives and marginal students. In M. C. Wang and M. C. Reynolds (Eds.), *Making a difference for students at risk* (pp. 119–155). Thousand Oaks, CA: Corwin Press.

Schubert, W. H. (1986). *Curriculum: Perspective, paradigm, and possibility.* New York: Macmillan.

Index

About the Author

Mark Perry is a teacher-educator and alternative high school teacher and principal. He works primarily with marginalized, dropout, and adjudicated students. He holds master's and doctorate degrees in education from the University of Illinois at Chicago. His teaching and research on race, cultural relevancy, white teachers, and alternative and democratic education are guided by the question: What is worthwhile to know and experience? He currently resides and teaches in Seattle, Washington, and can be reached for comments and responses at walkingtheline@hotmail.com.